SIGNS & SYMBOLS

WHAT THEY MEAN AND HOW WE USE THEM

SIGNS & SYMBOLS

WHAT THEY MEAN AND HOW WE USE THEM

A fascinating visual examination of how signs and symbols developed as a means of communication throughout history in art, religion, psychology, literature and everyday life

Richly illustrated with over 170 photographs and fine art paintings, together with 1000 black and white line drawings detailing some of the most important sets of signs and symbols

Mark O'Connell and Raje Airey

HERMES HOUSE

This edition is published by Hermes House, an imprint of Anness Publishing Ltd, Hermes House, 88–89 Blackfriars Road, London SE1 8HA
tel. 020 7401 2077; fax 020 7633 9499

www.hermeshouse.com; www.annesspublishing.com

Anness Publishing has a new picture agency outlet for images for publishing, promotions or advertising. Please visit our website www.practicalpictures.com for more information.

Publisher: Joanna Lorenz
Editorial Director: Helen Sudell
Editors: Joanne Rippin and Elizabeth Woodland
Artist (directory): Anthony Duke
Designer: Adelle Morris
Cover Designer: Balley Design Associates
Editorial Reader: Lindsay Zamponi
Production Manager: Steve Lang

ETHICAL TRADING POLICY
At Anness Publishing we believe that business should be conducted in an ethical and ecologically sustainable way, with respect for the environment and a proper regard to the replacement of the natural resources we employ.
As a publisher, we use a lot of wood pulp to make high-quality paper for printing, and that wood commonly comes from spruce trees. We are therefore currently growing more than 750,000 trees in three Scottish forest plantations: Berrymoss (130 hectares/320 acres), West Touxhill (125 hectares/305 acres) and Deveron Forest (75 hectares/185 acres). The forests we manage contain more than 3.5 times the number of trees employed each year in making paper for the books we manufacture.
Because of this ongoing ecological investment programme, you, as our customer, can have the pleasure and reassurance of knowing that a tree is being cultivated on your behalf to naturally replace the materials used to make the book you are holding.
Our forestry programme is run in accordance with the UK Woodland Assurance Scheme (UKWAS) and will be certified by the internationally recognized Forest Stewardship Council (FSC). The FSC is a non-government organization dedicated to promoting responsible management of the world's forests. Certification ensures forests are managed in an environmentally sustainable and socially responsible way. For further information about this scheme, go to www.annesspublishing.com/trees

Previously published as part of a larger volume,
The Illustrated Encyclopedia of Signs & Symbols

A CIP catalogue record for this book is available from the British Library.

PUBLISHER'S NOTE
Although the advice and information in this book are believed to be accurate and true at the time of going to press, neither the authors nor the publisher can accept any legal responsibility or liability for any errors or omissions that may be made.

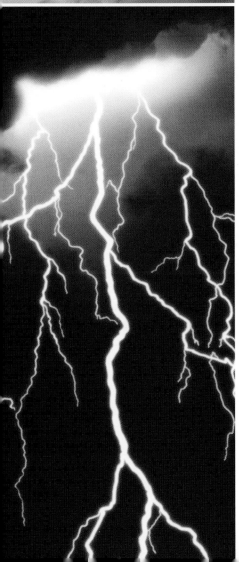

CONTENTS

INTRODUCTION

ABOVE The ancient Egyptian ankh is an early manifestation of the cross symbol.

The word "symbol" is derived from the ancient Greek *symballein*, meaning to throw together. Its figurative use originated in the custom of breaking a clay tablet to mark the conclusion of a contract or agreement: each party to the agreement would be given one of the broken pieces, so that when they reconvened the pieces could be fitted together like a jigsaw. The pieces, each of which identified one of the people involved, were known as *symbola*, so that a symbol not only represents something else but also hints at a missing "something", an invisible part that is needed to achieve completion or wholeness. Whether consciously or unconsciously, the symbol carries the sense of joining things together to create a whole greater than the sum of its parts, as shades of meaning accrue to produce a complex idea.

A sign, on the other hand, may be understood as something that stands for, or points to, something else in a more literal way. A sign exists to convey information about a specific object or idea, while a symbol tends to trigger a series of perceptions, beliefs and emotional responses. For example, as a sign, the word "tree" means a particular type of plant that develops a permanent woody structure with a trunk and branches, roots and leaves. As a symbol, the tree may have many meanings: it can represent fruitfulness and the bounty of nature, endurance and longevity or the web of family relationships; as a Christian symbol it can refer to the cross, and in many traditions it represents the "tree of life" that links the everyday world with the world of spirit.

Neither signs nor symbols have intrinsic meaning. The same tree can be described by many different words in different languages, and its meanings as a symbol are formed through human interaction with it. Both signs and symbols have become part of human social and cultural identity, changing and evolving as we do. They are vehicles for information and meaning, operating on many different levels – the universal and particular, intellectual and emotional, spatial and temporal, spiritual and material. They are a way of making sense of experience. If we could not classify the world using symbolic codes and structures we would be overwhelmed by sensory data. We need a way of describing what happens to us in order to understand it.

As well as being an essential part of human society, signs and symbols appear in nature, and may refer to pre-conscious information, as in the case of smoke signifying a fire nearby, or tracks signposting the presence of a particular animal. This book is primarily concerned with signs that have a conscious or unconscious meaning for humans, but as we are rooted in nature, we will see that there may be deeper connections between natural phenomena and the symbols that are meaningful to us.

While signs and symbols can serve as maps or pointers in everyday, or consensus, reality, the symbols of the dream or spirit worlds can help us to navigate the psychospiritual terrain of non-consensus reality. Spirits and dream figures are understood to guide us or compensate for some part of our wholeness as yet unlived. The significance of such symbols and signs fundamentally depends on our freedom to respond to them.

The ability to give meaning to signs and symbols led to the possibility of communication and reflection, and has enabled human beings to pass down their histories, mythologies and worldviews by means of storytelling, art and the written word. Signs and symbols have played a crucial part in furthering our scientific understanding of the world and have helped us to develop increasingly complex technologies, advancing from the invention of primitive tools to computers and spacecraft. Religious and spiritual traditions have used symbolism to help on the journey towards an understanding and experience of the divine and towards "right living". In psychology, approaches have been developed that use symbolism to work towards the alignment of mind, body and nature.

This book explores the use and power of ancient and spiritual symbols, whether they are for individual or social well-being. The first section, Signs of Life, provides an overview of the uses, meaning and development of signs and symbols as seen from a number of different perspectives: historical, cross-cultural, sociological and psychological. The reference section, Directory of Signs, contains more than 1,000 signs and symbols listed alphabetically, each with its own ideograph and a brief explanation of its meaning and application.

It is hoped that the information in this book will stimulate readers' interest in this profound and complex subject, prompting them to look beyond the superficial meaning of everyday objects and ideas to arrive at a greater understanding of the ways in which so much of daily life, and the way we communicate with each other, is informed by the richness of signs and symbols.

ABOVE The pyramids of Ancient Egypt symbolized for their architects the creative power of the sun and the immortality of the pharoahs who were buried inside them.

LEFT Mermaids, or sirens, are symbols of the alluring aspect of the female which has a powerful hold on the male.

BELOW The six-pointed star has great symbolic significance in many cultures, but is perhaps best known as the Star of David, an important symbol in the Jewish faith.

ABOVE Space, the planetary system of which Earth is a part, has had great symbolic meaning over the centuries. This is subject to change as science finds out more about the universe we exist in.

Signs of Life

Symbols are at the heart of cultural identity, informing every aspect of life. They draw on all sources – animate and inanimate – for their inspiration and appear in every conceivable form: as pictures, metaphors, sounds and gestures, as personifications in myth and legend, or enacted through ritual and custom.

Since the earliest times, the concept of symbolism has appeared in every human culture, social structure and religious system, contributing to every worldview and informing human understanding of the cosmos and our place in it. The great power of symbols has long been recognized: the ancient Chinese sage Confucius is said to have asserted that, "Signs and symbols rule the world, not words or laws."

RIGHT The monolithic statues on Easter Island have a life-like presence that symbolizes the steadfastness of the human spirit.

THE POWER AND MEANING OF SOME OF THE WORLD'S OLDEST SYMBOLS ARE STILL AVAILABLE TO US TODAY. FOUND IN THE SURVIVING ART AND ARTEFACTS OF THE WORLD'S EARLY CIVILIZATIONS, THEY SPEAK CLEARLY OF OUR ANCESTORS' PHYSICAL, SOCIAL AND SPIRITUAL CONCERNS, AND REPRESENT IDEAS THAT REMAIN FUNDAMENTALLY IMPORTANT TO MODERN HUMANITY.

PRIMORDIAL BEGINNINGS

ABOVE This Palaeolithic cave painting in Lascaux, France, was probably intended to create a symbolic link between the hunter and the bison, connecting him with the spirit of the animal.

BELOW The San Bushmen of the Kalahari desert still create rock paintings as symbolic visualizations of successful hunts.

Between the era of *Australopithecus*, the "Southern Ape" (from about 3.6 million BC) to *Homo sapiens sapiens* (25,000–10,000 BC), humans began to make tools, learned to use and then make fire, and constructed homes with hearths. They also began to use language, ritual and symbols.

What we know of our early ancestors comes from archaeological evidence such as cave paintings, artefacts and the traces of possible ritual practices, as well as comparisons with primitive peoples of later eras. Evidence of the development of symbol and ritual comes mainly from the Paleolithic people who emerged about two million years ago. They were hunters, and much of their industry involved working with chipped stone. During this era, the mythic imagination was stirred, and art began to be created.

The dawn of mythology and symbolism meant that people were beginning to relate to concepts deeper than just their daily existence. It is easy to imagine that their relationship with nature, the seasons and weather, the animals they hunted, the birth of their children and the inevitability of death led them to ponder the source and meaning of events in their lives. The primitive symbols of the cave, fire, the hand-axe, and the representation of animal figures, may serve as foundation metaphors for the complex human mythologies that have subsequently evolved. The symbols and rituals of primordial human beings may have served to align these people with the rhythms of their bodies and in nature, and to honour the forces influencing them.

THE MAKING OF FIRE

The ability to make fire and harness its energy was a highly significant development, achieved by *Homo erectus* (around 1.6 million–300,000 BC), and gave fire important symbolic qualities. The act of making fire represents the spark of imagination and creativity, and the energy of fire is in itself a symbol of power: harnessing and using nature to control other aspects of the natural world, bringing life-sustaining warmth, and frightening away threatening animals. Fire enabled people to extend the day after dark, creating a social time around a campfire or hearth, sharing myths and stories. At this early stage fire also became a symbol of transformation through the process of cooking.

CAVES AND CAVE ART

To primitive humans, caves were sacred places. People appear to have lived around or just inside the entrance, but ventured deeper into a cave only for religious or magical purposes.

Painting animals on the walls of caves may have been a means of connecting with their spiritual qualities. Boys were taken into the caves to be initiated as hunters – a rite that probably involved a symbolic death and rebirth, and which must have been a powerful experience, deep within a dimly lit, womb-like place surrounded by animal images.

To early humans a cave may have symbolized the leaving of everyday reality, as they went inside to find where their deeper

nature connected with and honoured the spirits of other animals; a place of transformation where they ritually died and were reborn in a new form.

Many early cave paintings, such as those of the Trois Frères cavern, in southern France, depict beings who are part-animal and part-human in form. A bearded male figure, with the ears of a bull, antlers and a horse's tail, may have represented either a divinity or a magician.

It is hard to differentiate between images of human magicians and divine figures in Palaeolithic art, as both appear to share this mixture of human and animal features. The magician was an important member of the community, and was probably considered a god in human form, with influence upon the gods and animal spirits.

HUNTING MAGIC

Palaeolithic humans certainly used magic to help in hunting animals. The principal form of magic was mimetic: they would imitate an animal they were hunting to connect to its spirit and ensure success. However, they also used sympathetic or homeopathic magic, in the belief that an act upon an object representing the animal would literally have an effect on the animal itself. Thus clay figures and drawings of animals that have been cut and slashed have been found, which were presumably to aid success in hunting.

A constant supply of game for the hunt was crucial, and fertility magic was performed to ensure it.

THE HAND-AXE

The stone-age hand-axe appears wherever early humans existed (except the very far east of Asia) and has been the most popular form of tool during the last two million years. It is a multi-purpose tool used for scraping animal skins, cutting meat, digging holes, cutting wood, and possibly as a weapon of self-defence against animals or other humans. The making of these tools involved chipping flakes from a "core" stone, signifying spiritual and psychological renewal of the core essence. Early two-faced axes are also thought to represent the repairing of interpersonal conflict.

This usually involved depicting a mating pair of animals, or females with offspring. Clay models of bison in couples and a bull following a cow have been found in France; at La Madeleine a drawing shows a doe with a fawn.

MAKING OFFERINGS

The earliest evidence of probable offerings to supernatural powers was found in the Drachenloch, in the Tamina Valley, in Switzerland. Bear bones had been placed there with some flesh still attached to the skulls, brains intact, and some leg bones, in a state as if to be eaten. They are thought to have been offerings to appease the animal spirits, to thank them for a successful hunt, and to seek favour with them for future hunting expeditions.

BURIAL

Palaeolithic finds include the first evidence of burial for sacred purposes. The dead were believed to gain supernatural powers, and would have been respected and referred to for guidance. Red ochre was sprinkled over the bodies; this may have represented blood and symbolized life and strength for the journey into the other world.

In Les Hoteaux, in Ain, France, a late Palaeolithic skeleton was found in a small trench, covered with red ochre. There was a large stone behind its head, and buried

with it were flint tools and the staff of a chieftain made from horn and engraved with a stag. Numerous other examples of bodies have been found in stone tombs or shallow graves, together with valuable jewellery, tools and other ritual objects. It seems the dead were being given food and tools, perhaps symbolically, to equip them for their existence in the next world.

Sometimes buried bodies have been found to have been tied up in a doubled-up position. This may have been intended to stop the dead from returning and tormenting their living descendants. In China the remains of human beings at an evolutionary stage halfway between *Pithecanthropus* and Neanderthal humans were found: apart from their skulls and lower jawbones, the other bones of the bodies had been placed to represent the animals they would have eaten. Did this ancient funerary ritual mean "You are what you eat"?

ABOVE Depictions of the sun and moon are centred on a human figure in this Venezualan engraving.

ABOVE Early people made ritual use of red ochre, used to stain this stone found in Bevoc, Bohemia, from 250,000 years ago.

BELOW As a symbol, fire is associated with creativity, destruction and imagination.

THE CRADLE OF CIVILIZATION

ABOVE We can only imagine what the early cities of ancient Mesopotamia looked like. This artist's impression shows a city's towering ziggurat to the left of the picture.

BELOW The law code of Hammurabi, 18th century BC, is an example of cuneiform script, the first written signs to replace pictorial representations.

As early hunter-gatherer societies found ways to work the land, more permanent settlements began to appear, particularly in areas where crops would flourish. One such area was in Mesopotamia, the "Fertile Crescent" of land between the Tigris and Euphrates rivers in what is now southern Iraq. From around 5000 BC small farming villages in the region were gradually developing into towns and cities, giving birth to some of the earliest civilizations – the word "civilization" comes from the Latin *civis*, which means "citizen of a city". People were inventing written languages, building temples, palaces and dwellings, and creating complex societies in which signs and symbols were interwoven with the fabric of daily life.

RECORD KEEPING
The ancient civilization of Sumer had thriving agriculture, trade and industry and was one of the first civilizations to develop a system of writing. Initially pictographs or icons were used, with one of the earliest

dictionaries containing about 2,000 graphic symbols, each one meant to resemble that which it represented. However, as society developed and the need to record complex matters increased, the limitations of pictorial representation became apparent. Gradually people realized that written signs could be used to represent sounds rather than things, and so pictures were replaced by cuneiform script, a written code based on a series of wedge-shaped characters, usually inscribed on to a soft surface, such as clay.

RELIGIOUS LIFE
The flooding of the Tigris and Euphrates was violent and unpredictable: from one day to the next, life-giving rain could change into an agent of devastation. It was believed the gods controlled these powerful forces, with humans little more than slave subjects to the whims of fate. This put religion firmly at the centre of daily life, with a temple dedicated to one of the major gods at the heart of each town or city. Initially these were

fairly simple mud-brick constructions, decorated with cone geometrical mosaics and frescoes with human and animal figures. A rectangular shrine, known as a "cella", had a brick altar or offering table in front of a statue of the temple's deity. Public rituals, food sacrifices and libations took place on a daily basis, as well as monthly feasts and annual celebrations of the New Year.

ZIGGURATS
These early temple complexes gradually evolved into ziggurats, towering pyramid-like structures, some reaching as high as 90m (300ft). One of the earliest examples from the region is the White Temple of Uruk (Erech in the Old Testament), dedicated to the Sumerian god An, lord of the heavens, dating back to the late 3000s BC.

Mesopotamian ziggurats were built in a series of three, five or seven increasingly narrow terraces, with steps for climbing to the next level. The seven terraces are said to correspond to the seven planetary Heavens. According to a Sumerian tradition, the bottom level was linked with Saturn and was painted black; the second level was white and corresponded to Jupiter; the third was brick-red and symbolized Mercury, while the fourth, blue level was associated with Venus. The sixth level, Mars, was yellow, while the seventh level was grey or silver to represent the moon, upon which the golden light of the sun would shine. Sacrifices were usually

RIGHT A winged bull with a human head, one of the hybrid mythological creatures known as lamassu that were carved into important public buildings in Assyrian cities.

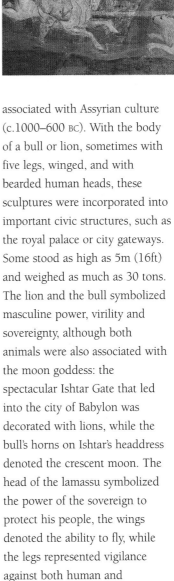

made at the top level. The symbolism of the ziggurat has also been compared with the cosmic mountain alleged to lie at the centre of the world, as well as with temples built in the shape of mountain. Symbolically, ziggurats are similar to ladders, joining Heaven and Earth and creating a passageway for mortals to ascend and the gods to descend. Ziggurats were allegedly the inspiration for the Tower of Babel, which in the Old Testament was interpeted as a symbol of pride built by humans attempting to equal God's splendour.

THE GODDESS ISHTAR

Arguably the most important deity in ancient Mesopotamia was the moon goddess, Ishtar, also known as Inanna, Astarte or Ashtar (and later, in ancient Egypt, as Isis). Ishtar personifies the forces of nature that can give and destroy life, and, like the moon, her form is ever-changing. Sometimes she was represented as a large-breasted, round-bellied fertility goddess. She is the goddess of sexual love, and in the homes of ancient Babylon little shrines containing her image showed her nude, seated in a window frame – the typical pose of the prostitute.

Ishtar is also the goddess of war, and in this aspect she could be depicted standing on a lion (symbolizing ferocity) and with the talons and wings of an owl. She was also shown wearing a three-tiered crown of stars, blue lapis lazuli stones and a rainbow necklace, symbolizing her connection with the sky. As queen

of the heavens, each night she rides across the sky in a chariot drawn by lions or goats. The zodiacal constellations were known to the ancient Arabs as the Houses of the Moon, and the whole zodiacal belt was known as the "girdle of Ishtar", a term that referred to the moon calendar of the ancients.

BABYLON

In ancient Babylon, the lion was a popular symbol of royal power, while the dragon was associated with the supreme god, Marduk. The laws and customs of the land were unified under Hammurabi (r.1792–1750 BC), and the city of Babylon became a renowned centre for learning, especially in science, mathematics and astronomy. Babylonian scholars developed a numbering system, based on groups of 60, which led to our 60-minute hour and 360-degree circle. The ancient Greek historian Herodotus declared that Babylon "is so splendid, that no city on earth may be compared with it". Its walls and famous hanging gardens were among the seven wonders of the ancient world, and Babylon became synonymous with excellence and attainment. In the Judaeo-Christian tradition, however, it became the antithesis of paradise and the heavenly Jerusalem, and symbolized the profane.

LAMASSU

Symbols of power and protection, massive winged sphinxes, or lamassu, have their roots in Babylonian magical traditions, although they are more usually

associated with Assyrian culture (c.1000–600 BC). With the body of a bull or lion, sometimes with five legs, winged, and with bearded human heads, these sculptures were incorporated into important civic structures, such as the royal palace or city gateways. Some stood as high as 5m (16ft) and weighed as much as 30 tons. The lion and the bull symbolized masculine power, virility and sovereignty, although both animals were also associated with the moon goddess: the spectacular Ishtar Gate that led into the city of Babylon was decorated with lions, while the bull's horns on Ishtar's headdress denoted the crescent moon. The head of the lamassu symbolized the power of the sovereign to protect his people, the wings denoted the ability to fly, while the legs represented vigilance against both human and supernatural enemies who could attack from any direction.

ABOVE This artist's impression of Babylon shows the popular sport of lion hunting. The lion was a symbol of royal authority and power for the Babylonions.

BELOW An impression of one of the towers of the Ishtar Gate of the city of Babylon, which was elaborately decorated with golden lions.

ANCIENT EGYPT

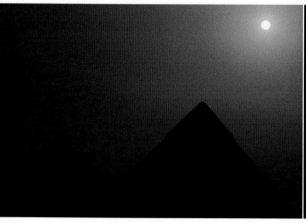

ABOVE The Egyptian pyramids hold a wealth of symbolism.

ABOVE MIDDLE The Double Crown of ancient Egypt had many symbolic associations, linking the two kingdoms of Upper and Lower Egypt.

PYRAMIDS

The pyramid is a symbol of ascension: erected in alignment with the sun and stars to create a passageway between Earth and the Heavens by which the dead pharaoh could cross to the afterlife. In the Western hermetic tradition, the pyramid combines the symbolism of the square with the triangle. The symbolism of the pyramid is also linked with the mound (and cosmic mountain), thought to resemble the hill that emerged from the primeval waters when the earth was created, so a symbol of the power of life over death.

In its prime, the civilization of ancient Egypt was arguably the most spectacular on earth. It emerged about 5,000 years ago and continued to flourish for three millennia, giving us a fascinating array of symbols, many of which were rooted in the land and nature. Ancient Egypt existed in a landscape of extremes, referred to in symbolic terms as Red and Black. The Red Land (Deshret) was the Saharan side of the country, made scorched and barren by the fierce heat of the sun; the Black Land (Kemet) was the fertile area in the Nile valley, darkened by the river's seasonal floods and shaded by its vegetation. In this way, the land of Egypt came to symbolize a marriage of opposites, a synthesis. This view informed the Egyptians' belief systems and lay at the heart of their culture.

ORDER AND CHAOS

The relationship between order (*maat*) and chaos (*isfet*) was at the crux of ancient Egyptian thought. The god Horus was associated with all that was right and ordered, and Seth with chaos, as well as infertility and aridity.

Similarly Kemet was a place of order – at the same time each year the Nile, Egypt's lifeblood, flooded the land, ensuring bountiful harvests – while Deshret was associated with infertility and disorder. Harmony was achieved when these two forces were held in equilibrium, neither gaining control at the expense of the other, and was personified by the goddess Maat, daughter of Re, the creator god and pre-eminent solar deity.

Maat was represented wearing an ostrich feather, symbol of truth and an ideogram of her name, on her head. She maintained order on Earth and in Heaven, ruling over the seasons, day and night and the movement of the stars, she also decided the fate of the dead in the underworld, weighing the deceased's heart against the feather of truth in her scales of justice. When the scales balanced, paradise was the reward; when they tipped, the deceased was devoured by a monster, part-lion, part-hippopotamus, part-crocodile. Maat also presided over decrees, legal acts and social relationships, and regulated religious rites.

ABOVE The Nile symbolized the lifeblood of Egypt, as the land's fertility was, and is, dependent upon its seasonal floods.

DIVISION AND UNIFICATION

Politically, the kingdom was divided into two parts: Upper and Lower Egypt, with Upper Egypt being in the south, and Lower Egypt in the north in the Nile Delta region – a division represented by the white and red crowns. The red crown of Lower Egypt had a tall, thin back and a narrow coil at the front, while the white crown of Upper Egypt was shaped like a tall cone with a bulbous tip. It was sometimes adorned with two plumes in a form called the atef-crown, which was associated with Osiris, lord of the underworld. Sometimes both crowns were combined to form the Double Crown.

It was believed that the origins of the state of Egypt could be traced to an act of unification of Upper and Lower Egypt by a ruler named Menes (for whom there is no actual archaeological evidence), around 3100 BC. The hieroglyphic sign used to express this notion of unification was a

THE ANKH

Formed by a loop over a T-cross, the ankh was the ancient Egyptian hieroglyph for life and immortality and was often used in the iconography of opposites. The loop, a form of circle, may stand for the universe (the macrocosm), and the T-cross for man (the microcosm). Alternatively, it combines the male and female symbols of the god Osiris (the T-cross), and the mother goddess Isis (the oval), sister and wife of Osiris, and symbolizes the union of Heaven and Earth. In Egyptian wall paintings, gods (particularly Isis) and kings are depicted holding the ankh, to symbolize their powers over life and death. The ankh is also associated with death and funerary rites: carried by the dead, it signals a safe passage between this world and the next, while held upside down, it is the key that unlocks the gates of death into eternity. Sometimes it is seen placed on the forehead between the eyes, linking it with clairvoyance.

stylized rendering of a pair of lungs, with a windpipe extending straight upwards from between them. In artistic representations, this emblem might be flanked by two deities, sometimes Horus and Seth, or on other occasions two Nile gods, one with a papyrus plant (the heraldic emblem of the Delta) on his head, and the other with the lotus (or waterlily) plant (the emblem of the Nile Valley). The figures on each side are often depicted tying the papyrus and lotus stems in a knot around the hieroglyph. It was the role of the king, or pharaoh, to unite these two lands, with his titles of "Lord of the Two Lands" and "King of Upper and Lower Egypt".

THE PHARAOH

The term pharaoh (*per-aa*) literally means "great house". In the New Kingdom period (c.1550–c.1069 BC) it was used to describe the king, but before that time it referred to the king's palace or the royal court. In ancient Egypt the king, or pharaoh, was believed to be a living manifestation of divinity, associated with both Horus, the falcon-headed sky god, and Re,

sometimes represented as a winged sun disc. This god-like status gave the pharaoh absolute power, having control over the army and all civil appointments, as well as the priesthood. Everywhere they went, ordinary people were reminded of the pharaoh's status, symbolized by massive stone statues of the king in the guise of Re, as well as the majestic pyramids – the funerary monuments of the kings and queens of ancient Egypt.

THE AFTERLIFE

Death and burial had many symbolic associations in ancient Egypt, where the existence of an afterlife was at the heart of religious belief. The practice of mummification reveals the strongly held belief that the body was required to be intact for life after death, while funerary texts show that the dead were believed to ascend to the heavens, the realm of the sun and place of the afterlife. There were several methods of ascent, including riding on the back of a falcon, goose or other bird; being wafted upwards with burning incense; or travelling on a reed float or barque that was sailed, rowed or towed. The journey was hazardous, and spells and recitations were uttered to help

the deceased on their way, while protective funerary amulets were positioned on the dead body.

Two of the most widely used amulets were the protective Eye of Horus (also known as the udjat or wadjat eye), which in one version of the myth of Osiris is used by Osiris's son, Horus, to bring his father back to life, and the scarab, which was placed over the heart. The scarab beetle was associated with Khepri (an aspect of the solar deity, Re) and was therefore a symbol of new life and resurrection. Sometimes scarabs were depicted with falcon's wings, as a symbol of transcendence and protection.

ABOVE The practice and ritualistic elements of mummification were full of symbolic meaning.

BELOW The Eye of Horus (wadjat) gives protection to a funerary barge on its way to the afterlife.

THE CLASSICAL AGE

ABOVE In antiquity, a laurel wreath was a symbol for victory, as well as a sign of status worn by the ruling classes.

Both the classical Greek civilization and the mighty Roman Empire have had an enormous impact on Western society, influencing its laws and customs, its art and science, its philosophy and way of life. The belief systems of these Mediterranean peoples can be seen in their mythologies, which were characterized by a vivid, dramatic vitality that enshrined the moral principles, natural laws and the great contrasts and transformations that determine both cosmic and human life. The gods and goddesses of the Greco-Roman pantheon acted out archetypal themes such as birth, death and renewal, war and peace, love and marriage, and governed all aspects of daily life.

The highest peak in the landscape of ancient Greece was Mount Olympus, home to the gods. From here they presided over the world and helped or hindered humans according to their whims. All the gods were thought to be descendants of Gaia (the Earth) and Uranus (the sky), and their lives were thought of in human terms – they fell in love, had children, played music, quarrelled and had affairs. Each of the gods had their own sphere of influence – Aphrodite (Roman Venus) governed love, and Ares (Mars) war, for example – and all the major deities had temples and sanctuaries dedicated to them.

CENTRE OF THE WORLD

One of the most important sanctuaries was the main shrine of Apollo at Delphi on the slopes of Mount Parnassus. Apollo, who in one of his aspects was associated with the sun, had the power of prophecy and divination, and at Delphi he would reply to questions about the future through his priestess. Delphi was thought to be the centre of the world, the point where two birds flying from opposite ends of the earth met. A huge stone, known as the *omphalos* or navel-stone, was placed there to symbolize this.

THE SUPREME GOD

The greatest god was Zeus (Jupiter to the Romans), who was the supreme ruler of Heaven and Earth as well as dominating the lesser Olympian gods. He was married to his sister Hera, but had many other sexual liaisons, fathering offspring of both goddesses and mortal women, typically while in disguise – taking such forms as a swan, a bull, a horse or a shower of gold. His symbols were the thunderbolt and eagle, although he was also depicted in human form wearing a crown of laurel leaves, seated on a throne and holding a sceptre.

TEMPLES

The earthly homes of the gods were their temples, and no expense was spared in their construction. Early wooden structures gave way to stone, especially marble, and they were decorated with brightly painted friezes showing the exploits of gods, goddesses and heroes. Most temples were dedicated to a particular deity, whose cult was centred on the location.

One of the most famous temples of ancient Greece, the Parthenon, was built on the Acropolis ("the high city") in Athens between 447 and 432 BC. It was dedicated to the city's patron deity, Athene, goddess of wisdom and warfare, and housed a huge gold and ivory statue of her. The owl, symbolizing wisdom, was her emblem and can be found on silver coins issued in Athens after the Greeks won decisive victories against the Persians in 479 BC.

The Romans' custom of deifying dead emperors meant that many temples were built to worship them, including that of Augustus and his wife Livia, which still stands in Vienne, France. Such temples were symbols of both divine and worldly power, testimony to the cultural and political achievements of the Romans.

SEASONS AND CYCLES

Greek life was dominated by religion, and this was inherently bound up with nature's cycles. The annual death and rebirth of the Earth's vegetation took symbolic form in the myth of Persephone (whom the Romans called Proserpine), the virgin daughter of Zeus (Jupiter) and Demeter (Ceres) the Earth Goddess. According to the myth of Persephone, Hades (Pluto, lord of the underworld) spied the beautiful maiden picking poppies and abducted her to be his queen in the realm of the dead. Consumed by grief, Demeter neglected the land while she searched for her daughter. The earth became barren as crops withered and died, and the result was perpetual winter.

To help humanity, Zeus intervened and sent Hermes (Mercury), the messenger god, to bring Persephone back. Meanwhile, however, she had eaten the food of the dead (in the form of six pomegranate seeds) and so was bound to Hades: she could be restored to Demeter for only part of the year. Her annual arrival is marked by the rebirth of spring but at the end of summer, she must return to Hades and the earth once again becomes barren.

GAMES

Not just for entertainment, sport was a way of training for warfare and of honouring the gods. National festivals attracted athletes from all over the Greek world, the most important being the Olympic Games, held every four years in honour of Zeus.

The Games were so important that wars were suspended to allow people to travel in safety to and from Olympia. The first Olympics were held in 776 BC and continued into Roman times, coming to an end in the late 4th century AD. They were revived in the modern era in 1896. One of the symbols associated with the Olympic Games is a runner bearing a torch, harking back to the time when relay races took place after dark, and the runners carried torches to light the way. The winning team used them to light fires on altars dedicated to Zeus or Athene. Winners wore laurel wreaths sacred to Apollo and a symbol of victory.

ABOVE The five rings that make up the symbol for the modern Olympic Games represent the five continents of the world.

BELOW Triptoleme, a prince of Eleusis, being initiated into the Eleusian Mysteries by Demeter and Persephone.

RIGHT The huge scale of the Colosseum was intended to impress both subject nations and Roman citizens with the Empire's immense power.

LAUREL

Through its association with Apollo, the aromatic leaves of laurel, or bay, were the crowning emblem of the Greco-Roman world for both warriors and poets. It was a symbol of truce, victory, peace, divination and purification.

BELOW The caduceus, a rod or staff entwined by two serpents, is a symbol of the god Hermes. It is used as an emblem for homeopathic medicine.

BELOW A she-wolf suckling the twins, Romulus and Remus, is one of the symbols for the ancient city of Rome.

MEDICINE AND HEALING

To the ancient Greeks, illness was seen as a punishment sent by the gods, to whom they also prayed for a cure. Sanctuaries dedicated to Asclepius (a Greek physician deified as the god of medicine) were set up all over the Greek world, the most famous being at Epidaurus. The sick made pilgrimages to such temples, where they practised a healing process known as incubation. They slept in the temple and used their dreams as a channel for communication with Asclepius, in the hope that he could show them how to get well. The priest would then carry out the recommended treatment. It was customary to leave some kind of symbolic representation of the afflicted part of the body, both when asking for healing and as an offering of thanks afterwards.

The emblem of Asclepius was his staff, a rough-hewn branch entwined with a serpent, whose shedding of skin symbolizes the renewal of youth. The staff is still

a familiar symbol of healing, and is used by medical bodies such as the World Health Organization.

The Romans also believed that illness could be caused by the gods, as well as by witchcraft and curses, and also left offerings to the gods in the shape of body parts. This practice continues in churches in some Mediterranean countries today, where embossed metal tokens are used.

THE FOUNDING OF ROME

According to legend, Rome was founded in 753 BC by the twin brothers, Romulus and Remus, sons of the Roman war god Mars. As babies, the twins were thrown into the river Tiber and left to die but were carried ashore and cared for by a female wolf. When they grew up, they decided to build a city on the Tiber. To decide where to build the city, each brother climbed a hill (Remus the Aventine and Romulus the Palatine) and sought omens from the gods. In the Greco-Roman tradition, the vulture was sacred

to Apollo and was a bird of augury. So when Romulus saw 12 vultures, while Remus saw only 6, the Palatine hill was chosen, and Romulus ploughed a furrow to mark out the city's limits. When Remus tried to take the initiative from his brother, Romulus killed him. Once Rome was established, Mars carried Romulus away in his chariot to become a god.

With its valour and predatory nature, the wolf was held sacred to Mars and became a totem symbol of Rome, one of the world's greatest superpowers. The Roman empire was built on the strength of its army.

POWER AND VICTORY

Based on rigorous discipline, iron will and courage, the Roman army became synonymous with the might of Rome. The army not only extended the empire's frontiers but also was responsible for its protection, building impenetrable hilltop fortresses to defend Roman gains. The goddess Nike, a winged aspect of Athene, became the symbol of military

victory. She was often shown with a globe and a victor's wreath, and sacrifices were made to her before and after battles to ensure victory and give thanks for success.

The eagle was adopted as the Roman standard. Known as the *aquila*, the standard itself became an emblem of imperial power. The eagle's wings sheltered the peace of the empire, while the bird's capacity to fell its victim in one deadly swoop was a reminder of Rome's warrior-like virtues.

Slaves were one of the spoils of war, and some (including women) trained as gladiators, who fought each other, often to death, in amphitheatres erected all over the empire. Public architecture of this kind, a powerful symbol of Roman domination, culminated in the building of the spectacular Colosseum in Rome. Opened in AD 80, it held about 50,000 people, and it has been estimated that 500,000 combatants died there. Gladiatorial fights had a religious origin, having been held at funerals to honour the dead, but by the time of the emperors

they were a bloodsport. The victors could win their freedom, and some gladiators achieved celebrity status – a graffiti inscription at Pompeii describes one called Celadus as "the man the girls sigh for". When a gladiator was wounded he could appeal for mercy. If the crowd (and the emperor) favoured him, the thumbs-up sign spared his life, while a thumbs-down sign signified a brutal death.

THE CULT OF MITHRAS

Originally a Persian sun god, Mithras achieved cult status with the Roman army, which spread his worship throughout Roman society and the empire. As creator and controller of the cosmos, Mithras was usually depicted slaying a bull, symbolizing man's victory over his animal nature, as well as Rome's political power over her enemies. Mithras was

worshipped in subterranean temples where the *taurobolium* (ritual sacrifice of a bull) took place, and initiates into the cult were baptized in its blood. Sometimes Mithras is depicted spanned by the circle of the zodiac, possibly alluding to the end of the age of Taurus and the beginning of the age of Aries pertinent to the time.

ABOVE Winged Victory – or Nike, an aspect of Athena to the Greeks – holds two of the most important Roman symbols of power and victory, a staff with an eagle on top and a wreath made of laurel leaves.

ABOVE LEFT The standard of a Roman legion was the ultimate symbol of its pride and military honour.

RIGHT In the ancient Roman empire, the cult of Mithras was open to men only. This frieze depicts the god slaying a white bull, symbolizing male sexual potency and power in its purest form.

PAGAN EUROPE

ABOVE An instrument of the soul, the Celtic harp was said to have inspired three responses: happy laughter, tears of sadness, and serenity or sleep.

THE CELTIC SWORD

To the Celts, the sword symbolized power, protection, courage, authority, truth and justice. The sword is also a phallic symbol. Some swords were thought to possess magic qualities. The image of Arthur drawing the sword from the stone after others had failed was a sign of his royalty.

When Rome and its western empire fell to barbarian invaders in AD 476, northern Europe entered a period of instability. The influence of Roman civilization receded, though classical learning was preserved in Christian monasteries, and the old Celtic culture was interwoven with the Germanic and Scandinavian traditions of the incoming forces.

In the 6th century the Anglo-Saxons reached Britain from Scandinavia and Germany, displacing Roman, Celtic and Christian culture from what now became the "land of the Angles", or England. Later, between 800 and 900, the Vikings raided mainland Europe and Britain. By the 11th century, however, the new cultures had been assimilated and Europe rose re-formed out of the Dark Ages into the Middle Ages, with the flourishing Roman Christianity as the dominant faith, blended with elements of the older, pre-Christian cultures.

THE CELTS

Celtic myths and symbols were passed down by the bards, who blended the roles of priest, teacher and entertainer and kept the culture alive. The Celts had a deep affinity to nature, and natural patterns feature strongly in Celtic art.

In County Galway in Ireland stands an ancient standing stone, known as the Turoe stone. It is carved with stylized patterns suggestive of plants and animals, and is a symbol of regeneration. It may have been a place where ageing kings were sacrificed for cultural renewal.

The Celtic cauldron was an important symbol of abundance, rebirth and sacrifice: an unending supply of food or knowledge, often associated with the supreme Celtic god Dagda. The dead, thrown into the cauldron, were said to be reborn the next day. The Celtic cauldron may be a precursor of the Holy Grail of the Arthurian legends. A magnificent gilded silver and copper cauldron of the 1st or 2nd century BC, the Gundestrup cauldron depicts Kernunnos, the "Horned God", a male animal deity, in a sacred marriage with Mother Earth, or nature. He bears the antlers of a stag, symbolizing renewal (as stags shed their antlers and grow new ones). He appears also with a boar, which the Celts admired for its speed and willingness to fight; they believed it had magical qualities and direct links to the underworld. Kernunnos holds a ram-headed serpent, symbol of sexuality and regeneration.

There are many examples in Celtic art of the triple goddess, appearing in her three aspects: maiden, mother and crone. Brigid was the triple goddess commonly associated with the Celtic spring festival of Imbolc, celebrated at the time of lambing. She inspired

ABOVE The Gundestrup cauldron displays a magnificent array of Celtic nature symbolism, including the horned god Kernunnos, an animal deity.

the bards and was a deity of healing who also protected women in childbirth.

Another triple goddess was Morrigan, who was associated with the crow. The consort of Dagda, she was a goddess of battle, strife and fertility. She had the power to make men completely helpless, in particular when they did not recognize their feminine qualities. Dagda's name means "the all-powerful god". He was a protective father-figure, often pictured holding a club, or with an erect penis, symbolizing virility and the creation of life.

The Celts worshipped their gods in sacred groves of trees. They began to build temples only when influenced by the Romans. The oak tree symbolized power and protection, and oak groves were sacred spaces.

THE ANGLO-SAXONS

Around AD 450 the Anglo-Saxons began their migration to Britain from Denmark and northern Germany. They were a proud warrior society, with polytheistic

beliefs, and worshipped animals such as the boar, horse and stag.

The Anglo-Saxons believed in a fixed destiny or fate, known as *wyrd*. The concept was embodied in the three Wyrd Sisters, or Norns, who wove the web of fate (rather like the Greek Fates who were believed to spin, measure and cut the thread of each human life).

Horses were sacred to the Anglo-Saxons, and represented great wealth and rank. Legends tell of Hengist ("stallion") and Horsa ("horse"), the twin gods who were said to have led the invasion of Britain. Huge chalk horses carved into the hillsides of southern England, such as those at Uffington and Westbury in Wiltshire, are thought to be Anglo-Saxon in origin.

The boar was an Anglo-Saxon symbol of protection and royalty. It was associated with Frô, a god of kingship and fertility. Warriors bore its image on their helmets, in the belief that this would make the power of the boar accessible to the wearer. At Yuletide, to mark the shortest day of the year, solemn vows were made over the

Yule Boar, which was then sacrificed: it was thought to go straight to the gods, taking the vows with it, while its carcass was roasted and served with an apple in its mouth, symbolizing the rebirth of the sun goddess.

The stag was a noble symbol for the Anglo-Saxon king and his leadership. A stag-pole, mounted with the head of a stag facing the sun, was customarily erected to curse or insult an enemy.

The festival of the fertility goddess Eostre was celebrated in spring, and she gave her name to the Christian festival of Easter. Her animal was the hare or rabbit – the origin of the modern Easter Bunny: according to one legend she transformed a bird frozen in a winter storm into a rabbit, which continued to lay eggs each spring in gratitude.

THE VIKINGS

The Norse people of Scandinavia, worshipped a pantheon of gods and goddesses led by Odin. The Vikings were seafaring Norse warriors and traders who flourished from the 8th to the 11th centuries, raiding Europe

from the sea in their mighty, longships, taking first belongings, and then territory, from the native Saxons.

Odin, or Wotan, the chief Norse deity, was the god of thought and memory, two mental faculties esteemed by the Norse peoples. Thor was the god of lightning and thunder, and thus of power, wielding a mighty hammer to protect humans and gods from giants. Freya was the goddess of love and beauty, but was also a warrior goddess; her sacred animal was the cat. Freya's twin brother was Freyr, a horned fertility god, god of success, and also a warrior god, fighting with a horn or an elk.

BELOW Viking longships were symbols of terror and ferocity to the unfortunate people who suffered the incursions of the Norsemen.

ABOVE The Anglo-Saxons associated the boar with kingship, plenty and protection in battle.

VIKING SHIPS

The Vikings were master ship builders and saw their sea vessel ("horse of the waves") as a symbol of power and speed. The ships were also potent symbols for safe passage to the afterlife, with ships used in burials, securely moored and anchored, protecting the corpse's body.

HELM OF AWE

Thought to make the wearer magically invincible and terrifying to his enemies, the Helm of Awe is a Viking symbol of protection. As well as being a physical helmet worn between the eyes, the Helm of Awe also probably refers to a form of magic practice used to create delusions in the minds of others.

THE MIDDLE EAST

Sometimes referred to as the crossroads of history – the meeting point of East and West – the Middle East saw the beginnings of civilization and was the birthplace of Judaism, Islam and Christianity. Its cultural complexity reflects its long history of human migration, conquest and trade.

THE PERSIAN EMPIRE

From the late 6th century BC the Persian Empire, the largest and best-organized empire the ancient world had hitherto seen, dominated the Middle East, embracing lands from the Mediterranean coast to the borders of India. The Persians unified for the first time the Iranian plateau, which became the new power centre of the region – an area that had been dominated culturally and politically by Mesopotamia and Egypt for most of the preceding 2,500 years.

A vast and mountainous area, the Persian empire contained many different peoples who often rebelled against Persian control. To keep order, the Persians had a very effective army of 10,000 specially trained men, bodyguards to the king and keepers of law and order who were feared wherever they went, moving quickly to put down rebellions. The members of this elite warrior force were known as the "immortals" because when one

soldier died, he was immediately replaced. Mosaics of the immortals carrying spears decorated the royal palace at Susa, the capital city.

ZOROASTRIANISM

In AD 247, the Sassanid dynasty established Zoroastrianism as the official religion of the Persian Empire, and it is still practised in Iran and other parts of the world. It is founded upon the teachings of the prophet Zarathustra (called Zoroaster by the Greeks), in which the opposing forces of good and evil are symbolized by Ahura Mazda, the supreme deity responsible for truth and light, and the evil Ahriman. The two represent the duality of the cosmos: unlike Satan, Ahriman is not a creation of the supreme god but his equal.

The universal conflict between good spirits (*ahuras*) and bad ones (*daevas*) will ultimately result in the triumph of Ahura Mazda, and the faithful are encouraged to follow Ahura Mazda through "good thoughts, good words and good deeds".

These three ideals are represented by the three wing feathers of the *faravahar*, a central Zoroastrian symbol. Zoroastrians believe that the first animal to be created was a white bull, the progenitor of all other animals and plants, while the focal point of the religion is fire, seen as the purest manifestation of Ahura Mazda. Perpetual fires were set up all over Persia, some in the open air, others enclosed in fire temples, and tended by priests known as magi (from which comes the word "magic"). Depictions of fire altars are found on ancient coins.

Because Zoroastrians consider fire to be sacred, cremation is disallowed because it would contaminate it; instead, bodies are exposed at the top of "towers of silence" for their bones to be picked clean by scavengers.

THE BEDOUIN

The Bedouin are the desert-dwelling nomads of the Middle East, many of whom preserve their traditional lifestyle to this day. Their name comes from an Arabic word meaning "inhabitant

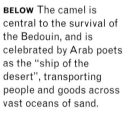

BELOW The camel is central to the survival of the Bedouin, and is celebrated by Arab poets as the "ship of the desert", transporting people and goods across vast oceans of sand.

RIGHT This winged device is the *faravahar*, a symbol of the human desire to achieve union with Ahura Mazda, the supreme deity of the Zoroastrian faith.

CARPETS

Throughout the Middle East, carpets are much more than functional objects, being used to symbolize important elements of tribal, family and personal life. Their patterns are rich in symbolic meaning. For instance, camels, the wealth of the Bedouin, signify happiness and riches for the weaver and owner of the carpet, while the peacock's wheel-like tail is a symbol of the sun and the cosmic cycle. It is customary for a carpet to contain a deliberate flaw, as only God can create perfection.

of the desert". They wear long, flowing robes to stay cool, but probably the most important aspect of a Bedouin man's attire is his headgear. This consists of a cloth held in position by the *agal* (rope), which indicates the wearer's ability to uphold his honour and fulfil the obligations and responsibilities of manhood. Bedouin women also signify their status with their headgear – married women, for instance, wear a black cloth, known as *asaba*, about their foreheads.

Traditionally the Bedouin are divided into related tribes, each led by a sheikh. Moving from place to place according to the seasons, and living in tents, they herd camels, sheep and goats, riding highly prized horses, famous for their grace and speed.

In such a harsh environment, any violation of territorial rights is viewed with severe disfavour:

BELOW Incense resins are precious substances with many different symbolic properties. Frankincense is used for purification.

small piles of stones are traditionally used to mark property boundaries. On the other hand, in the silence and solitude of the desert, encountering another person can be an unusual and noteworthy event. This has led Bedouin culture to place great value on hospitality and social etiquette: visitors are greeted with music, poetry and dance. Throwing frankincense pellets on the fire is a traditional greeting.

PRECIOUS INCENSE

One of the best-kept secrets of antiquity was the location of the trees that produced myrrh and frankincense, valued more highly than gold. Fantastic stories surrounded their whereabouts: the Greek historian Herodotus wrote that they were guarded by winged serpents who would kill any who tried to take their resins, and the wealth of the legendary Queen of Sheba was said to have been built on these substances. In the desert lands of Arabia,

frankincense and myrrh were rich in symbolic associations. Together with gold, they have always been associated with royalty and divinity. Incense has a long tradition of use in sacred ceremonies, its swirls of fragrant smoke viewed as a flight path for prayers and communion with the gods. Frankincense is associated with masculinity and the spirit of the heavens myrrh is feminine and linked with the earth.

ABOVE The black head-cloth worn by Bedouin women is a sign of their married state.

TOP Many of the everyday trappings of Bedouin life have symbolic meaning, including this man's tent and clothes.

TRADITIONAL TENTS

The tent is the abode of the desert nomad and has many symbolic associations. In the Old Testament, the wandering tribes of Israel set aside a tent (or tabernacle) for God, which became the prototype for the temple. Like the temple, the tent is a place to which the godhead is summoned to make itself manifest. In many traditions, the tent's pole is linked with the symbolism of the pillar and column (as well as the tree), representing the connection between Heaven and earth. Bedouin tents symbolize the duality of male and female. They are usually divided into two sections, one for men, one for women, by a curtain known as a *ma'nad*. The men's area is called the *mag'ad* (sitting place) and is for the reception of most guests. The *maharama* (place of the women) is where the women cook and receive female visitors.

TRIBAL AFRICA

ABOVE A Tongan shaman from Zambia sits in his grass hut with various gourds, animal horns, and other symbolic items spread before him.

A land of deserts, savannah, high mountain ranges and dense, equatorial rainforests, Africa is a vast and diverse continent. It is home to many different social systems, where more than 1,000 languages are spoken and where myths and cosmologies are interlinked with moral codes and ways of seeing the world.

Although it is impossible to come up with a homogeneous view of African culture, it is fair to say that for thousands of years, the way of life for many Africans has changed less than in more industrialized parts of the world, and that traditionally people have made their living by herding, hunting or farming. Symbols in African religion, art and culture reflect this social and historical continuity, and in most African societies the spiritual world and natural world is reflected in everyday life.

SPIRITUAL BELIEFS

In many traditional African societies the spiritual world and the everyday world are one and the same, with all aspects of life permeated by a strong power or vital force. In some societies this is seen to emanate from a supreme creator spirit – the Masai of Kenya call him Ngai, while the Nupe in Nigeria say that their god Soko is in the sky, for instance. There is often a hierarchy of spirits, from the nature spirits of rivers, rocks, trees and animals, through ancestor spirits of the dead, to divinities who derive their power from the creator spirit. The Lugbara of Uganda have a cult centred on the spirits of the dead, in which the living are considered to belong to the "outside" world while the dead belong "in the earth". If the ancestors are neglected, the dead punish their descendants by inflicting misfortune and sickness.

It is widely believed that spiritual power can be manipulated for good or bad. Positive mystical power is productive, can cure illnesses, and is protective, while negative power eats the health and souls of its victims and causes misfortune. A variety of specialists such as witch doctors, medicine men and women (known as *nganga* in most Bantu languages), diviners and rainmakers possess knowledge of this power and use it in the making of "medicines". Medicines may be used to encourage or prevent rain from falling, to aid hunting, for protection against malign spirits, for success in love affairs, or to find stolen property.

They may also be used for treating illnesses. Medicines can be made from almost any material, but natural materials such as trees, plants and animal skins or feathers are common, and are fashioned into amulets and charms with symbolism that varies according to the materials used and the purpose for which it was created.

MASQUERADE

Among traditional African societies, masks are used for many different social events and rituals, particularly those surrounding initiation ceremonies and rites of passage. Combined with a costume to hide the identity of the wearer, the role of the mask has many functions, both spiritual and temporal. Masks are worn to inform or educate, discipline or lend authority, to give the wearer access to special powers, or simply to entertain. The role of the mask is communicated through movement and dance – masquerade – where the complete costume becomes a powerful and energetic force that represents both the human and spiritual world. Masquerade is often performed by men who are members of secret societies: among the Dogon of Mali, for instance, the men's secret society or *Awa*, organizes all funeral events, with masked dancers in funeral processions. The masks have strong symbolic meaning, and the dancers represent figures of male and female powers and figures from the animal world, and the afterworld.

In traditional Yoruba society, women are considered to have two distinct sides to their nature, the power to create and nurture life, coupled with the potential for great destruction. Among the Yoruba, the Gelede masquerade, danced in either male or female pairs, is supposed to ensure that women's power is channelled for the benefit of the community. Gelede masks come in many different designs and are usually worn on top of the head, adding greatly to the wearer's height.

Whatever their purpose, all costumes and masks are highly stylized creations, their symbolism varying depending on the context. Among the Ogoni of Nigeria, many masks are designed to look like animals, with the wearer assuming the spirit or character of the mask and performing athletic displays in imitation of the animal he represents. Many masks are highly elaborate constructions: the Sande female initiation society of the Mende of Sierra Leone have a wooden mask decorated with carvings that represent ancestors who preside over the initiates.

ADINKRA SYMBOLS

The art of adinkra – symbols hand-printed on cloth – is characterized by symbolic motifs, graphically rendered in stylized geometric shapes. The symbols relate to the history, philosophy and religious beliefs of the Ashanti people of Ghana and the Ivory Coast and are grouped into various categories, including creatures, plant life, celestial bodies, the human body and non-figurative shapes. Initially used for funerals, the cloth is now worn for many other occasions, providing the symbols are appropriate, and is itself seen as a symbol of the Ghanain culture.

BELOW The masks of the Dogon form a line, symbolizing connection between the sun and Earth through the conduit of the dancer's body.

BELOW Adinkra cloth was originally specially made for funerals. Its name translates as "saying goodbye to one another".

ABOVE LEFT Akoben, the adinkra symbol for vigilance and wariness.

ABOVE RIGHT Gye Name, meaning "except for God", is the most popular adinkra symbol of Ghana.

SOUTH AND SOUTH-EAST ASIA

ABOVE The Chinese emperor, dressed in symbolic yellow, in front of a dragon-motif screen.

ABOVE The Japanese Flag, showing the "sincere" red sun on a "pure" white background.

KOI CARP

The Japanese Koi carp found swimming in many Japanese water gardens are symbols of the patience, courage and strength required to achieve big goals in business and life.

The cultural, political and spiritual history of East Asia has been rich and dramatic, and it is a huge reserve of symbolism, stretching from the ancient traditions to modern times. Great civilizations had been established in India by 2500 BC and in China by 2000 BC. Japan viewed itself as the "third kingdom", equal to China and India, and by tradition was founded in the 7th century BC by the Emperor Jimmu, whose imperial dynasty continues unbroken to this day.

EMPERORS

Far Eastern emperors have long associated themselves with elemental and mythical sources of power. Nippon, the Japanese name for Japan, means "the land of the rising sun", and the imperial family emphasized its central role in the country – and its authority – through the use of solar symbolism. Japanese emperors, through their legendary ancestor Jimmu, traced their ancestry back in a direct line to the great sun goddess, Amaterasu,

the central deity of the Shinto pantheon. The imperial seal was the chrysanthemum, a symbol of the sun and the national flower of Japan. In modern Japan the emperor continues to occupy the chrysanthemum throne: the long unbroken dynasty symbolizes continuity with the past, and the emperor is constitutionally defined as the symbol of the state.

Emperors in China were the rulers of the Middle Kingdom (the everyday world) and the Four Directions, maintaining harmony between Heaven and Earth. They had nine insignia: the dragon, mountains, the pheasant, rice grains, the axe, flames, pondweed, the sacrificial bowl, and patterns symbolizing justice.

The dragon is symbolic of imperial power and the emperor's role in mediating between Heaven and earth. It appeared on the Chinese national flag during the Qing dynasty, and was embroidered on court robes. The Chinese believed themselves to be the direct descendants of the Yellow Emperor, who was said to have the head of a man and the body of a dragon. Yellow, symbolic of the Earth and therefore of farming, remained the imperial colour. From the Han dynasty (206 BC–AD 220) onwards, dragons were also depicted in other colours, each with different symbolism: the turquoise dragon became the symbol of the emperor, connected with the East and the rising sun.

In 1950 the Indian government adopted, as a national symbol, a sculpture from the reign of Emperor Ashoka (r.272–232 BC).

This pillar of carved stone depicts four lions, an elephant, a horse, a bull, and another lion, all separated by a lotus at the base with the inscription "truth alone triumphs". The sculpture is founded upon the wheel of law or dharmachakra, which symbolizes the teachings of the Buddha.

ARCHITECTURE

The Great Wall of China is a universal visual symbol for China. It snakes its way across the country's entire northern boundary and was completed by the Qin emperor Qin Shi Hang as a means of defence against barbarian tribes from the north. Thousands of slaves died during the building of the wall, which led to it becoming a symbol of tyrannical oppression.

During the Ming dynasty (1368–1644 BC) the wall was refortified in the grand style seen today, and it is considered one of the seven great wonders of the world. From various perspectives it can be seen as a symbol of power, division, closed attitudes and oppression.

In India near the city of Agra, the Taj Mahal is an enduring and profound symbol of love. Completed in 1652, this magnificent tomb was built by the Mogul emperor Shah Jahan, in memory of Mumtaz Mahal, his favourite wife, who had died in childbirth. Centrally sited among canals and tranquil gardens, the tomb is built of shimmering white marble, embellished with semi-precious stones. The four canals in the gardens symbolize the four rivers of Paradise described in the

Qur'an, while the gardens represent the final resting place for the souls of the dead.

The Taj Mahal was erected as a symbol of love, but perhaps also as a demonstration of Shah Jahan's greatness. It is said that he planned a second mausoleum for himself, built in black marble on the opposite side of the Jamuna river and connected to the first by a silver bridge, but he died before his plan could be carried out and was buried in the Taj Mahal.

RICE AND TEA

Throughout Asia, rice is a staple food, generally associated with abundance, prosperity and fecundity, a symbol of life. The Balinese, who eat rice at every meal, refer to it as *nasi*, meaning "nostril": in other words, eating rice is seen to be as important as breathing. In China, girls with poor appetites have been told that every grain of rice they do not eat will be a pockmark on their husband's face.

In Japan rice is seen as sacred, and the eating of rice as a sacred ritual. Offerings are made to the Shinto deity Inari, the bearer of rice. The Japanese believe that soaking rice prior to cooking releases life energy, which can bring peace to the soul. Sometimes rice grains are referred to as "little Buddhas" to encourage children to eat them.

In India, rice is considered an auspicious food. The new crop is celebrated as part of the festival of Pongal, when it is cooked in pots until they overflow. People decorate the ground in front of their homes with coloured rice

flour and make offerings to the gods. It is said that grains of rice should be like two brothers, close but not stuck together. At Hindu weddings the couple hold rice, oats and leaves, symbolizing health, wealth and happiness.

In China, tea is served to a guest as a symbol of respect and goodwill, and refusing a cup of tea is considered rude. The teacup is filled only seven-tenths full, the other three-tenths being filled with friendship and affection. According to legend, tea drinking began when the emperor Shen Nung rested one day in the shade of a tea plant, and several leaves tumbled into his cup of hot water. Upon drinking the golden liquid a wonderful sense of well-being came over him.

Green tea was taken from China to Japan by Zen Buddhist monks, who drank it to keep

RIGHT The fabulous Taj Mahal, an Indian emperor's passionate symbol of his eternal love for his princess, Mumtaz Mahal.

them awake while meditating. The Japanese elevated the drinking of tea to an art, in the form of a Japanese tea ceremony, or Chanoyu, which embodies elements of Zen philosophy. The Chaji tea ceremony consists of up to five hours of ritual movement.

THE LOTUS

Although it grows in the mud, the lotus maintains its beauty. As India's national flower it is a symbol of pure spirit rooted in mundane reality. The Buddhist mantra "Om mane padme" refers to enlightenment, the "jewel in the lotus".

LEFT The Great Wall of China is an example of how one thing can have diverse symbolic meanings, depending on one's cultural or political perspective. The wall is variously seen as a symbol of protection, power, and achievement, or of oppression, isolation and division.

ABOVE A mask from the Malay Archipelago (New Guinea) using elements that link the human world with the natural one.

TOP Polynesian canoes are intricately carved, symbolizing spiritual power and prestige.

The thousands of islands in the central and southern Pacific Ocean, including Australia, New Zealand, Polynesian Hawaii and the Malay Archipelago, together make up Oceania. There are three major cultural groupings: Polynesia, Melanesia and Micronesia. The indigenous people of Australia are another important cultural grouping from this area.

INDIGENOUS AUSTRALIANS

"Aborigine" is a Western term used to describe indigenous people who have been conquered or colonized by Europeans. The indigenous people of Australia have occupied the country for over 60,000 years, probably coming originally from the Malay Peninsula. Their spirituality is intimately linked with their relationship with the land through the "Dreamtime".

The Dreaming is a vital concept of creation. It refers to the creation of the earth, humans and animals, but at the same time it is eternally present on a mythical level. All life is believed to be imbued with the Dreaming. Dreamtime stories portray the Ancestors moving through the earth, shaping the land, and giving life to plants and animals. Through the Dreamtime the Aboriginal people and the earth are part of one another. The individual tries to live his or her life according to the law laid down by the Ancestors.

As the Spirit Ancestors journeyed through the land, they created dreaming tracks, often called "songlines", as they sang the land into life. The aboriginal peoples believe that by singing specific songs, at key points on the land, they directly connect with the Dreaming.

Totem animals play an important part in aboriginal society. Clans have a totemic relationship with a specific animal, and it is taboo for them to eat the meat of that animal, as it would be like eating a close relation. The characteristics and qualities of the totem animal become accessible to the clan. Some Australian Aboriginals still adhere closely to the Dreaming of their totem. One man whose totem was the cockatiel was allowed to travel the world because the nature of the cockatiel was to fly over borders.

POLYNESIA

Encompassing much of the eastern area of the South Pacific, with the major islands of Hawaii and New Zealand, Polynesia was one of the very last areas in the world to have been populated, mostly in waves of migration.

Although the islands are widely separated, Polynesian societies have a thread of unity running through their belief systems and social structures. These are aristocratic societies, led by chiefs. The nobility are thought to have spiritual power, known as "mana", which is brought out through ritual and art.

The Polynesian sculptor brings out the mana in his or her art by revealing the beauty and essential qualities in the wood or stone. Ornamental carvings appear on spears, canoes, jewellery, house beams and on many other kinds of domestic and spiritual objects. Tiki Man is a male figure found throughout Polynesia, in wood sculptures, carved in stone, and in tattoo and clothing designs. He is believed by Polynesians to be their first ancestor or the original human, and symbolizes the phallus or procreative power.

Carvings made by the Maori of New Zealand, in bone, shell, jade and wood, depict important mythological themes and patterns in nature. The *koru* represents the fern frond, a symbol of new life and purity coming into the world. The twist is a vertical form in which two spirals interweave. This represents eternity and the eternal relationships of couples or cultures. *Hei-matau* is a stylized fish-hook, representing prosperity and abundance and a deep respect for the ocean. It is a symbol of power and authority and is said to give the wearer protection when travelling at sea.

The huge Easter Island statues are carved in stone, and probably represent guardian gods, facing inwards towards the island peoples. The oversized head in Polynesian sculptures highlights the sacred attributes of the head.

POLYNESIAN TATTOOS

There are two kinds of Polynesian tattoo. *Enata* are natural symbols that refer to the individual's life, origin and social rank. They also protect the wearer: a fisherman would have designs that would protect him against sharks, while a warrior's tattoos would defend him against attack. *Etua* are

mystical symbols referring to past ancestors – a lineage of shamans, chiefs and divinities. These symbols showed mana, which was passed down the lineages.

MELANESIA AND MICRONESIA

There are many cultures and over a thousand languages in Melanesia and Micronesia. The Papuans were the first inhabitants of Melanesia, arriving at least 40,000 years ago. Traditional society is based upon agriculture, the domestication of pigs, hunting and trade.

Melanesian religious art usually displays brilliant colours and is made from a broad range of materials. Much religious artwork honours and placates the powerful influences of animal and nature spirits, as well as showing respect for the ancestors. It often consists of a network of human, animal and natural images. Effigies of the totem animal of a

BELOW The Rainbow Serpent appears in aboriginal paintings up to 6,000 years old.

clan, such as a fish, snake or crocodile, sometimes show the animal devouring a clan father. Although this looks sinister, it probably indicates the spiritual identification of the people with their totem animals. For the Latumul people of New Guinea, the saltwater crocodile is the creator of all things. It is said that Crocodile, who was the first human being, mated with a crack in the ground (the first woman) to engender life. The lower jaw of Crocodile became the earth and the upper jaw the sky. The people believe that, during initiation, boys are swallowed by Crocodile and regurgitated as men.

Respect for the ancestors is important for the Melanesians, as they are thought to influence the living relatives. Much symbolic art is aimed at maintaining a good relationship between the earthly and the spiritual realms. The wearing of masks is one important way of honouring and depicting the ancestors. The masks of north central New Guinea depict supernatural spirits and ancestors. Made from an array of shells, animal skins, seeds, flowers, wood and feathers, these masks are understood to be a dwelling-place for the spirit, and a great source of strength in business and in warfare.

In traditional Vanuatuan society the human–pig relationship is of intense importance, to the extent that when a pig is slaughtered it is sung to and caressed before and during its death. Pigs are believed to have souls and may be considered family members. The number of pigs owned relates to the leadership status of the owner, as does the length of their tusks. When pigs feed naturally the tusks wear down and, to avoid this owners feed them by hand. The pig is also a sexual symbol, embodying the relationship between men and women.

ABOVE The Easter Island statues are symbols of religious and political power, and are believed to be repositories for sacred spirits.

ABOVE The *koru*, a Maori fern spiral, represents the unfolding of new life.

BELOW The crocodile is an honoured totem animal in many Oceanic cultures.

RAINBOW SERPENT

The Rainbow Serpent is central to the beliefs of the people of Arnhem Land, but is found in aboriginal art throughout Australia. It is a large snake-like creature associated with the waterways of Australia. It represents the source of life and protects the people and the land, but if not respected it becomes destructive.

CENTRAL AND SOUTH AMERICA

ABOVE RIGHT A temple relief shows the Mayan Jaguar god conducting a blood-letting ritual with his wife, Lady Xoc.

ABOVE The jaguar is a central motif throughout Central and South America, frequently associated with deities.

BELOW The markings on the ancient giant Sun Stone are symbols linked to Aztec cosmology.

At the time of the Spanish conquest in 1519, great urban civilizations existed in Mesoamerica – controlled by the Maya and Aztecs – and the central Andes region – under Inca rule. The foundations of these civilizations were laid by earlier cultures such as the Olmec, Chavin, Nazca and Toltec, and shared many features: monumental architecture, ceremonial centres with pyramid and plaza complexes, complex calendrical computations and – for the Maya – hieroglyphic writing. The art and culture of these civilizations was rich in symbolism, linked especially to the natural world.

THE JAGUAR

Once known as the people of the jaguar, the Olmec worshipped gods that were half-human and half-animal. The jaguar was their most favoured and feared deity. Admired for its strength, ferocity and hunting ability, the jaguar was one of the most powerful symbols in both Mesoamerica and South America, and its stylized form appears on artefacts throughout the region. Gods were often portrayed wearing the jaguar's skin as a sacred costume, and the cat was venerated as the divine protector of royalty by both Maya and Aztec rulers. The supreme Aztec god and patron deity of royalty, Tezcatlipoca (Lord of the Smoking Mirror), was said to possess an animal alter-ego in the form of a jaguar, which inhabited mountain summits and cave entrances. According to Maya mythology, copal resin, one of the most important and sacred incense-burning substances of the ancient American cultures, was a gift of three different jaguars, white, golden and dark, corresponding to the three different colours of the resin.

CALENDARS

A calendar is a symbolic representation of time. It is a way of pinpointing the regular recurrence of natural phenomena – such as the rising and setting of the sun – against which human events can be set. The Maya used two calendars of different lengths,

one sacred, one secular; dates were calculated on the two planes of existence concurrently. The two calendars were so complex that the same juxtaposition could not recur for 374,440 years.

The great Aztec calendar stone (also known as the Sun Stone) is the largest Aztec sculpture ever found. Measuring 4m (13ft) in diameter, its markings were more symbolic than practical and relate to Aztec cosmology. The Aztecs believed that the world had passed through four creations, which had been destroyed by jaguars, fire, wind and water. The sun, moon and human beings were created at the beginning of the fifth and current creation, which is predicted to be destroyed by earthquakes. The calendar stone was used to calculate such danger periods. At its centre is the face of the Earth Monster, surrounded by symbols of previous creations. Twenty glyphs representing the names of each day in the Aztec month occupy the innermost circular

ABOVE This Aztec carving of their ritual ballgame shows a decapitated player (right): the blood streaming from his neck is shown in the form of snakes, which were symbols of fertility.

band. Each day the sun god had to be fed with human hearts and blood to give him strength to survive the night and rise again.

HUMAN SACRIFICE

Religious rituals involving human sacrifice formed part of the Inca, Aztec and Maya traditions. Human sacrifice was a symbol of communion with the gods, particularly the sun, rain and Earth deities. For the Aztecs and Incas, these bloody acts took place in temples or on mountains, while the Maya sometimes sacrificed their victims in wells. The Aztecs usually sacrificed their captured enemies, and it is said that in one four-day period of great celebration, some 20,000 victims were killed. Men, women and children could all be chosen.

The Aztecs preferred to stretch out their victims over a sacrificial stone and pluck out the still-beating heart; this symbolized the most precious organ that could be offered to the gods and replicas

were sometimes made in jade.

Prized more highly than gold, jade was a symbol for life and agriculture. Ritual vessels thought to be for the blood or hearts of sacrificial victims were often decorated with skulls, a symbol for fame and glory, or else defeat, depending on the situation. Human skulls were sometimes made into masks and used in ritual performances.

THE BALL COURT

For the Mayas and Aztecs every aspect of life, including sports, revolved around religion. In particular, the Mesoamerican ball game *ulama* had a sacred symbolism. Only nobles could play the game, in which two teams of two or three players aimed to propel a small, solid rubber ball through rings in order to score points. The rings were variously decorated, sometimes with snakes and monkeys. The ball-court represented the world, and the ball itself stood for the moon and the sun. The game was fiercely competitive, as the losing team was often sacrificed; it represented the battle between darkness and light, or the death and rebirth of the sun. It was also

believed that the more the game was played, the better the harvest would be.

NAZCA LINES

More than 1,000 years ago perfectly depicted giant figures, including animals such as a hummingbird, a whale, a monkey and a spider, were carved into the coastal desert floor near Nazca in southern Peru. Some are so large that they can be appreciated only from the air. It seems likely that they had some kind of sacred significance, perhaps as offerings to the mountain and sky gods.

ABOVE Maya numbers, from top, left to right: 0, 1, 4, 5, 11 and 18. The Maya number system used 3 signs – a dot for 1, a bar for 5 and the shell for 0. Other numbers were made by combinations of these signs.

NATIVE NORTH AMERICANS

ABOVE White sage is a sacred herb that symbolizes purification, and is often used in North American rituals.

MIDDLE The eagle stands for power and vision.

TOP The quadrated circle of the Medicine Wheel, symbol of the earth.

FAR RIGHT Many Native American peoples revered the bison as a symbol of power and good fortune.

BELOW The bear represents both power and healing to the Native Americans.

The indigenous peoples of North America probably came from Asia 12,000–25,000 years ago via the Bering Strait. Waves of migration from Alaska to the east and south led to a large number of different tribes or linguistic families populating seven major cultural areas: the Arctic, the North-west Coast, the Plains, the Plateau, the Eastern Woodlands, the North and the South-west. A commonly understood sign language was developed among these people, who were often on the move and sometimes at war. The arrival of Europeans, from the 15th century, led to huge population collapses from imported diseases to which the indigenous people had no immunity. Many wars also took place between the Native Americans and the expanding white community.

The Native Americans were shamanic societies who lived in a close spiritual relationship with the land. Their lifestyle was adapted to various ecosystems, sometimes sedentary and sometimes nomadic, with an emphasis on hunting, gathering, fishing or agriculture. Their history and relationship with nature inform the mythologies and symbol systems that appear in the art, music and rituals of these peoples.

THE MEDICINE WHEEL

Sometimes known as the Sacred Hoop, the Medicine Wheel is an important representation of Native American spirituality, but is also conceived as a living entity in which humans and nature are interrelated. The Medicine Wheel

is a circular model in which the individual or culture orientates itself with all aspects of nature on the journey through life.

The Native Americans believe that the Great Spirit created nature in the round. The sun and moon are round, circling around us and marking circular time. The sky is a circle and the horizon is the edge of Mother Earth, from where the four winds blow. Each year is a circle divided by seasons, and the life and death of an individual is also seen as a circle.

The wheel is a quadrated circle, with the four directions and the four sacred colours marked upon it. Each direction represents particular natural and animal powers and the qualities that go with them. The eagle is found flying in the east and is a symbol of vision, endurance and strength. The mouse and innocence may be found to the south, the bear and introspection to the west and the buffalo and wisdom to the north. In addition to these four are three more directions: Father Sky (above), providing rain and warmth for things to grow; Mother Earth (below) the source of life-sustaining plants and animals; and the sacred fire at the

centre, where the people are attached to the Great Spirit.

To the Native American, "medicine" means power, a vital energy force in all forms of nature. The individual is placed on the wheel at birth, with certain perceptions and medicine powers, and as they walk their path on the wheel they acquire medicine power or wisdom from new perceptions and aspects of nature.

ANIMAL MEDICINE

Bison medicine was often seen as a representation of the feminine principle of the nourishing and life-giving force of the earth. The bison was considered to be the chief over all animals of the earth. Bear medicine has male aspects of strength and power, as well as more feminine aspects associated with knowledge of healing using roots and herbs, and introspective qualities related to hibernation.

The eagle is the lord of all birds and holds the greatest power. Eagles, and birds in general, are thought to have a very similar spirit to humans, as they fly in circles, with circular nests, and are not bound to the earth like four-legged animals. The eagle embodies great vision and

overview, and a tremendous power to overcome all enemies and to strike with impeccable intent. When worn, the eagle feather is a reminder that the Great Spirit is present: the eagle is associated with the sun and its feathers with the sun's rays.

TOTEM POLE

The Algonquin word *totem* means a person's personal guardian, usually an animal or plant by which the Native American is adopted through a rite of passage at adolescence.

The totem pole is carved, often out of cedar, and is both a family or clan emblem and a reminder of their ancestors. It is a symbol of dignity and accomplishment, the historical and spiritual rank of the people. Many of the symbolic meanings and stories associated with the images are known only to the people of the clan. For example, the stories of the North-west Pacific Coast tribes tell of the transformation of animals into humans as wel as humans into animals. The salmon or whale people are said to live in great happiness in cities beneath the waves. Thunderbirds are said to dive from the sky, snatching huge whales for their dinner. Wolves, becoming tired of hunting on the land, become killer whales and hunt in the sea.

THE CORN GODDESS

Corn, or maize, originated from a wild grass called *teosinte*, which grew in southern Mexico 7,000 years ago. The Native Americans selectively cultivated corn, and once the Europeans arrived, corn

RIGHT Eagle feathers on the headdresses of Native American chiefs symbolize the sun's rays.

agriculture quickly spread to the rest of the world. As a staple food, corn has inspired many important myths. It is said to be one of three sisters, Corn Woman, Squash Woman and Bean Woman, goddesses of fertility.

The Iroquois corn goddess (Onatah) is the daughter of Mother Earth (Eithinoha). Onatah is caught by spirits from the underworld, and must be rescued by the sun so that the crops can grow. Similar stories relating to the seasons are found in many agricultural societies.

THE VISION QUEST

An individual seeking guidance or answers to questions may embark on a vision quest, a ritual practice through which helpful signs may be given, which can be interpreted as guidance from the spirits. Vision quests occur when an adolescent makes the transition to the path of adulthood. The seeker asks the shaman for help. A remote site in nature is found and marked out with a rectangle or circle, where the seeker waits for a vision. Sacred offerings such as tobacco (which blesses the earth) are placed within this area for the Great Spirit. Sometimes sage, the purification herb, is laid on the ground as a bed for the seeker. The seeker stays in the sacred area for one night or several, praying and awaiting signs from the world around. The Great Spirit might speak through any experience, even insignificant encounters with animals and birds or other forces in nature. Eventually thanks are given to the

Great Spirit for what has been given, and the seeker shares the experience with the shaman to gain understanding.

THE GIVE-AWAY

Potlatch is a Chinook word for a "give-away" ceremony in which prominent people give a feast and give away their possessions, redistributing them among the tribe. Sometimes at the end of the ceremony they burn down their house and become poor, until they build up their wealth again.

Giving is important to the Native American, who considers it a great honour on the part of the one who gives and for the one who receives. One should share one's wealth and never hold on to more than is needed. The turkey is thought of as the give-away or earth eagle. The turkey is a free-spirited bird of sacrifice, opening the channels to others.

ABOVE The totem pole is carved with figures and faces placed on top of each other. They represent ancestors or supernatural beings encountered by clan members, or who have given them special gifts.

ARCTIC TRADITIONS

ABOVE The Arctic is known as the land of the midnight sun.

ABOVE For the Innuit the igloo is a symbol of home and family life. In Canada it is a registered trademark for the Inuit.

BELOW Some of the symbolic tools of the Inuit: the box top, *kepun* axe and the *cavik*, a curved knife.

Within the Arctic Circle, a large ocean is surrounded by land, with tundra at its fringe and animal, human and plant life throughout the area. The Arctic includes Siberia and other parts of northern Russia, Alaska in the United States, northern Canada, Greenland, Lappland in Finland, northern Norway and Sweden. It is peopled mainly by the Inuit of Alaska, Canada and Greenland, and the Finno-Ugrians of northern Scandinavia and Siberia, which include the Saami.

The ecology, climate and geology of the Arctic influence the signs and symbols of its peoples. The Arctic is known by the people who live there as the "land of the midnight sun": in the summer the sun never sets, and in the winter it never rises. The taiga and tundra are featureless landscapes with wide horizons, a good home for reindeer or caribou, and thus suit nomadic cultures that rely on reindeer for food. Seal hunting, whaling and saltwater fishing are also important to human survival.

INUIT SPIRITS

The name "Inuit" means "the real people": the Algonquin named them "Eskimos", meaning "raw flesh eaters". Inuit spirituality is concerned with conciliating the gods and nature spirits, to help humans survive in harsh conditions. Unseen forces in nature are called *innua*, and they can be found in the air, water, stones and animals. The *innua* can become totemic guardians of men, known as *torngak*.

Stone and bear spirits are considered particularly powerful. When a bear spirit becomes a man's *torngak*, he is symbolically eaten by the bear and reborn as a sorcerer or *angakok*.

The *innua* of animals are thought to be very sensitive to the craftsmanship of the weapons by which they are killed. If they were killed by a poorly made tool they would report this to the spirit world, and the animal spirit might not return to earth in another animal body. To avoid this the Inuit take great pride in their craftsmanship.

THE IGLOO

The word igloo means "dwelling", and the *igluvigaq* is the ice dwelling used by the Central Inuit in the winter. Constructed from upward spiralling blocks of ice, the igloo walls curve inwards, creating an ice dome with a hole for ventilation in the top.

The igloo is a symbolic extension of those who built it and their relationship with their surroundings. The igloo is built from within, and once the "keystone" has been placed at the top, the igloo and its builder become one. The igloo enables the Inuit to survive harsh conditions, and is built from the very elements of that extreme environment.

In Inuit mythology, Aningan is a moon god and a proficient hunter who has an igloo where he can rest in the sky, when not being chased through the sky by his brother the sun. He shares the igloo with Irdlirvirissong, his demon cousin, who sometimes comes out to dance in the sky making people laugh.

The igloo symbolizes a resting-place and psychic home for different facets of human nature. In 1958 the Canadian government registered the image of the igloo as a trademark to protect the work of Inuit artists and woodcarvers.

SYMBOLIC TOOLS

Two other important items in Inuit culture are the *inuksuk* and the *ulu*. A common symbol in northern Canada, the *inuksuk*, means the "likeness of a person" in Inuktitut. It is a signpost guiding the Inuit through the featureless tundra. Made from rock, *inuksuk* appear as human forms with their legs outstretched, and often serve the purpose of guiding caribou into places where they can easily be captured. The longer arm of an *inuksuk* points the hunter in the appropriate direction. If an *inuksuk* points towards a lake, it is an indication that fish can be found in the lake at the same distance the *inuksuk* stands from the edge of the lake.

The *ulu* is a woman's knife with a crescent-shaped blade, used for cutting out clothing, preparing skins, and in cooking. The *ulu* is a symbol of femininity and the woman's role in Inuit society.

THE COSMIC TENT OF THE SAAMI

Formerly known as Lapps, the Saami are part of the Finno-Ugric race, a large group of tribes speaking many different dialects of one parent language. The Saami were traditionally hunters and fishermen, who also farmed domesticated reindeer; since the reindeer have been dying out, they have become more nomadic.

As an essentially shamanic culture, the Saami conceive of a world with different levels of reality: the lower world, the middle world and the upper world. The world is imagined to have been constructed as a kind of cosmic tent, with the central pole of the World Tree reaching up from its roots in the lower world, through the middle world of everyday life, to the upper world constellation of the Great Bear at its top. The central pole is also described as a four-sided world pillar.

The sky is thought to have been fixed in place by the "north nail", the Pole Star, and prayers ensure it stays in place so that the sky does not fall down. The Saami are concerned that the Pole Star might one day move, leading to the destruction of the earth.

The traditional Saami dwelling is a conical compound tent or *kata*, a predecessor of the yurt, capable of withstanding very strong winds and snow. It is a symbolic map of the cosmos, with the hearth at the centre, the skin of the tent representing the sky, held up by wooden supports equivalent to the world pillar.

Within the *kata* there is a sacred area where the sacred drum is kept. The Saami also believe that when a member of the family dies the body should be taken out of the tent through the *boasso* (or kitchen) side, otherwise someone else will die.

REINDEER

The reindeer has central importance within Saami culture, and reindeer herding is a symbol of personal, group and cultural identity. Saami children are often given a "first tooth" reindeer and a "name day" reindeer, and more reindeer are given to them at their wedding, so that a new household is usually equipped with a small herd of reindeer with which a couple can start their new life together. The reindeer is also often associated with moon symbolism and with funerary ritual and passage.

ABOVE The reindeer is an all-encompassing, multi-faceted Saami symbol of life and death. It is believed to conduct the soul of a dead person to the upper world.

KALEVALA

Elias Lönnrot, a Finnish scholar, collected the mythic and magical songs passed down orally by generations of peasants, and published the *Kalevala*, the Finnish national epic, in 1835. Its poems and sagas offer important insights into the beliefs and traditions of the Saami peoples.

SACRED DRUM

The sacred drum is important to the Saami. Constructed from birch, with a drum head of reindeer skin, the drum is commonly painted in alder juice or blood with figures of people, the nature spirits and the four directions around a central symbol of the sun. A series of small rings moves as the drum is beaten, and where they eventually come to rest leads to shamanic predictions and divinations. The Saami use their drum as a guide in daily life, to find things that have been lost, and for healing purposes.

SYMBOLS OF SPIRITUALITY

BOTH SIGNS AND SYMBOLS PLAY A VITAL ROLE IN ALL THE WORLD'S RELIGIONS AS OBJECTS ON WHICH THOUGHTS AND PRAYERS CAN BE FOCUSED. THEY POINT A WAY THROUGH THE NUMINOUS WORLD OF THE SPIRIT, ACTING AS BADGES OF FAITH, TEACHING TOOLS AND AIDS ON THE JOURNEY TOWARDS AN UNDERSTANDING OF COMPLEX PHILOSOPHIES.

SHAMANISM

ABOVE Seedpods are commonly used for making shamanic rattles.

BELOW A North American shaman, holding a drum and spear, "shape-shifts" into a wolf.

The ancient tradition of shamanism involves the individual entering altered states of consciousness to visit other levels of reality, from which teaching, healing or visions may come for his or her community. With its origins in the Palaeolithic period, shamanism may be found at the roots of many of the world's major religions, and at the fringes of many others.

The word *saman* comes from the Tungus of Siberia, and means "one who knows". Shamans are adepts of trance, an ecstatic and altered state in which they are thought to leave their bodies, ascending into the sky in "magical flight" or descending into the underworld, to meet with the ancestors and commune with nature spirits. Many of the symbols of shamanism represent transcendence or release from one way of being into another.

Traditional shamanism is now little practised, but a wave of interest has developed in the West, inspired by Jung's linkage of it with his ideas about the "collective unconscious", and a growing recognition of the importance of travelling between different worlds or states.

THE CALL OF A SHAMAN

Shamans may inherit their role, but more often they experience a spontaneous vocation in which they are called or elected by nature. The shamanic calling is itself a symbolic occurrence. Often an initiate is called by a near-death experience, such as being struck by lightning or surviving a life-threatening illness. Some have a lucid dream-like experience of dismemberment, whereby they metaphorically die and are then reborn.

Other shamans may be "called" by meeting a divine or semi-divine figure in a dream. Often these dream figures are the dead ancestors of the shaman who inform him that he is being elected. Some shamans have celestial wives by whom they are called to their path.

Facing your own death, or journeying into death, is powerfully symbolic of the shamanic ability to transcend the everyday self and to live impeccably in the face of the attacks and challenges of life. It is said that some shamanic warriors have become so centred that they can walk across a firing range without harm. Psychologically, the deathwalk is the ability to drop personal history and identity, so there is nothing to be attacked.

SHAMANIC FLIGHT

The shaman is said to be able to take magical flight in the form of an animal, or as a spirit detached from the body. In this way shamans can fly about the universe bridging Earth and the heavens, and many symbols reflect this.

Palaeolithic cave paintings at Lascaux, in France, show the shaman in a bird mask, and Siberian shamanic priestesses still wear bird costumes. In rock art of the San (Bushmen) of southern Africa, the *ales*, or "trance buck" is an antelope-like creature, with its legs raised in flight. It probably symbolizes the shamanic ability to

commune with the ancestors, since in San mythology the dead are transformed into elands. Similar flying animals occur in Siberian shamanic mythology (and may be the source of the flying reindeer of Santa Claus).

PARALLEL WORLDS

The basic shamanic cosmology consists of three levels or worlds – the upperworld, middle earth and the underworld – but some traditions describe as many as seven or nine different worlds.

The role of the shaman is to make links or travel between these worlds, and many symbols refer to the connection between them. In Native American traditions the smoke rising through the smoke hole of a tipi refers to the passage of spirit between earth and sky. The world tree is a shamanic symbol that occurs in many cosmologies – the Norse god Odin, who hangs himself on the world tree Yggdrasil, achieves knowledge through the altered state that results from his suffering. The ladder is a similar symbol, seen in the seven-notched birch trees of Siberian shamanism, but also in other traditions, such as in the Egyptian Book of the Dead and the Old Testament.

For many shamans there is a direct relationship between themselves and the natural world. A Romany shaman speaks of the earth as his grandmother, and the plants, animals, sun, moon and stars as his relatives, with whom he communicates for guidance. All of nature thus becomes a form of living symbolism. Some

RIGHT A Tungus shaman of Siberia wears the skin and antlers of his spirit ally, the reindeer, to deepen his relationship with the animal.

psychologists see a direct connection between the parallel realities of the shaman and the relationship between dreaming and everyday reality. From this perspective signs and symbols from the unconscious, or in nature, are doorways calling us into another level of reality. A dream about an eagle, for example, may invite us to take a detached overview, with sharp-focused attention.

THE DRUM

Used to induce a shamanic trance, the drum has particular symbolic significance as a vehicle into altered states or otherworlds. The repetitive rhythm played upon the drum, and sometimes on rattles or other instruments, blocks out other sensory information, enabling the shaman to enter a different state of consciousness. The drumbeat relates to the primal sound sometimes thought of as the heartbeat of the earth.

For the shamans of the Altai of central Asia, the drum skin stands for the division between the upperworld and the lowerworld. In all shamanic cultures the drum is symbolic of the relationship between the upperworld, often associated with the male, and the underworld or womb, associated with the female.

THE SHAMAN'S ALLY

A shaman has an ally or teacher in the form of an ancestor, a dead shaman, or often an animal or nature spirit, who helps them reach altered states and their deepest nature. It is through this

relationship that the shaman eventually encounters their double or individuated self. The shaman may imitate the actions and voice of an animal ally as a way of sharing their perceptions, gifts and intelligence. Saami shamans are said to become wolves, bears, reindeer or fish. The Tungus shaman of Siberia has a snake as a helping spirit and during the shamanic trance replicates its reptilian movements.

SHAMANIC JOURNEYS

The symbolic world of the shaman can be meaningful to people who suffer breakdowns or near-death experiences. The shaman can leave the present reality in order to find wisdom or knowledge in alternative realities. The helpful spirits of animals and ancestors may be seen as aspects of a person's unconscious, encountered on life's journey.

BELOW A shamanic drum with a stylized image of a running horse painted on its surface.

TAOISM

ABOVE The "all-powerful" seal of Lao-tzu, a Taoist magic diagram harnessing cosmic *chi*.

BELOW According to legend, Lao-tzu, saddened by people's inability to accept the "way" he proposed, departed from civilization and rode into the desert on a water buffalo. At the last gate of the kingdom he was persuaded to leave a record of his teachings, and wrote the *Tao Te Ching*.

Taoism is a religious and philosophical system, said to have been founded in China by the sage Lao-tzu (or "the old one") in the 6th century BC. Taoism was influential in China and Japan, and in modern times interest in it has also spread to the West.

According to tradition, Lao-tzu was the author of the *Tao Te Ching*, or "Book of the Way", a collection of aphorisms concerned with the nature of the world and the alignment of humanity to this nature. Its central principle is non-action – not passivity but an active responsiveness to the nature of life, an appreciation of life as it is, rather than striving to fulfil a succession of desires.

Both Taoism and Confucianism have been highly influential upon Chinese culture and history. Confucianism is an ethical approach to living and government based on fixed principles, rooted in the belief that civilization can build a better society, while Taoism is more concerned with living in accordance with the nature of things as they are.

THE TAO

Both a personal and a cosmological principle, the Tao (or the "way") describes the origins of the universe and creation. It refers to the source of nature's patterns and the ebb and flow of natural forces. At the same time, the Tao is a mystical path that can be followed by living in a state of simplicity, in accordance with nature's rhythms.

Whereas in the West the heart is seen as a source of courage or love, to the Chinese it is the source of sensation, the seat of the five senses. Discovering the Tao depends on "emptying" the heart of the ever-changing illusions of the senses, so that it is true and eternal. Lao-tzu is commonly quoted as stating that "the Tao which can be spoken is not the eternal Tao". This means that the Tao refers to that which precedes all manifest things (or "myriad things") in nature.

Whereas many religious systems view heaven as a state outside of the human earthly existence, Taoism, and much Chinese thinking, is more concerned with oneness, in which a person lives in and identifies with the Tao. Thus living according to the Tao means to be guided by the deepest path in nature, which lies between earthly and heavenly existence.

YIN AND YANG

For Lao-tzu there was no such thing as a fixed definition of good or evil, in that as soon as a state of "goodness" is described it immediately and inevitably invokes a balancing state of "non-goodness" as an opposing force. The yin/yang symbol is indicative of the balancing natural law or cycle of change, in which every movement contains or eventually turns into its opposite: strength leads to weakness, life to death, and male to female.

Yin, the female principle, is associated with coldness, darkness and the earth; yang, the male principle, with light, warmth and heaven. The symbol shows that life must be viewed as a whole and cannot truly exist in isolated parts. The dark and light parts of the symbol are directly opposed yet interlocking and mutually dependent; the two small spots in the symbol show that each opposing force contains the seed of the other. Together the two shapes form a perfect circle, symbolizing the wholeness of nature.

A contemporary example of this principle is evident in humankind's relationship with the ecology of the planet. Our ability to harness power, resources and information has grown enormously, but if we fail to recognize our dependence on the greater whole – the animals and forces of nature around us – our strengths will eventually bring about our demise. The yin/yang symbol shows how each force, when at its most powerful, gives rise to its opposite.

DIVINE FIGURES

Originally, Taoism had no static religious doctrines, nor was it involved in deity worship, but over time, as it became popular, it was mixed with older Chinese beliefs such as the theory of the five elements and the veneration of the ancestors. It became something more akin to a folk religion, and a whole pantheon of divinities was worshipped, including the mythical Jade Emperor. Lao-tzu himself was deified and became one of the most important Taoist gods.

The Taoist pantheon mirrors the imperial hierarchy in Heaven and Hell, and Taoist priests relate to these divinities through meditation and visualization. Sometimes for the general public, metaphysical or symbolic theatrical rituals have been devised to portray the meaning and workings of the divine hierarchy. Many Taoists pray to these divinities or make offerings at shrines devoted to them.

Lao-tzu is said to be one of the reincarnations of the Great Supreme Venerable Lord, or T'ai-shang Lao-chun. He is symbolic of one who has become one with the Tao, thus succeeding in the creation of an immortal body that separates from the physical body at death.

Yu-huang, the Jade Emperor, also known as the Lord of Heaven, is said to be the supreme ruler of the heavens and of the underworld. For the Chinese, jade symbolizes nobility, perfection and immortality, and is considered the "stone of heaven". The Jade Emperor is the chief administrator of moral justice and also the protector of humanity. In Chinese tradition, the heavenly administration was regarded as a replica of the emperor's government on Earth, and the Jade Emperor was in direct communication with the emperor of China.

P'AN-KU AND THE FIVE SACRED MOUNTAINS

Another important Taoist figure is the mythical P'an-ku, who is said to be the first created being. Upon the creation of the universe, in which Chaos was divided into the forces of yin and yang, the interaction of these opposing principles led to the creation of P'an-ku, who thereupon picked up a chisel and a mallet and began to carve the rest of creation, and in particular the space that lies between Heaven and Earth. P'an-ku lived for 18,000 years, growing every day, and when, on completion of his task he lay down and died, his body became the world, the extent of which was marked by the five sacred mountains of China. Symbolically linked to the five elements, these stood at the four cardinal points and in the centre of the empire, and were believed to support the heavens.

Lao-tzu advised his followers to "be still like a mountain and flow like a great river", and many have sought the Tao by retreating to live alone in the mountains. In Taoist belief, mountains are a medium of communication with the immortals and with nature. Like the image of the world tree, they link the worlds above and below. The sacred mountains are sites of pilgrimage. They have been worshipped as deities in their own right, monasteries cling to their slopes, and the emperor himself climbed annually to the summit of the holiest peak, Tai Shan, the mountain of the east, to offer a sacrifice.

ABOVE The Jade Emperor was revered as the divine head of the hierarchy of heaven and hell.

TOP The yin/yang symbol represents the endless interplay of opposing qualities in nature.

THE TAO AND THE MOON

According to some texts, the earliest Taoists were shamans who flew to the moon and there learned all the secrets of change. In contrast, the Taoist view of the sun was of something constant. These early Taoists were far more interested in what could be learned from the moon and its phases.

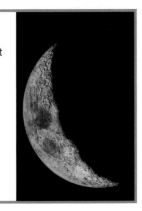

HINDUISM

ABOVE Ganesh, the elephant-headed god, symbolizes sacred wisdom and abundance.

ABOVE The four heads of Brahma represent the four directions.

With no single historical founder, no set of creeds or dogmas and no one source of authority, Hinduism encompasses a huge variety of beliefs and rituals, intricately woven into the land and culture of India. Of the world's major religions, Hinduism has the third largest number of followers (the majority of whom live in India and Nepal). Many Hindus, however, do not recognize the term Hinduism as a description of their religion, referring instead to *sanatana dharma* – the eternal religion or law. The complex Sanskrit word *dharma* refers to the natural unchanging laws that sustain the universe and keep it in balance, a similar concept to the Tao. It translates in daily life as an obligation to follow certain laws and to fulfil social and ethical responsibilities, so that for many Hindus there is no division between secular and religious life.

BRAHMAN

In Hindu thought, there is one ultimate Supreme Being – Brahman – who is infinite and eternal. Brahman is the source of life, the world soul, and is present in all things as the *atman*, the true self or the unchanging essence of the individual living being.

Just as all living beings represent tiny parts of the universe, so Brahman takes different forms, representing certain aspects of the divine. Consequently there are many gods and goddesses in the Hindu pantheon, including the elephant-headed Ganesh, god of good fortune and wisdom; Hanuman, the monkey god, representing loyalty, courage and devotion; and Lakshmi, the four-armed goddess of fortune.

THE TRIMURTI

The word *trimurti* means "having three forms" in Sanskrit, and is the term used to describe the supreme trinity of Hinduism: Brahma (the Creator), Vishnu (the Preserver) and Shiva (the Destroyer). Brahma the Creator (sometimes depicted with four heads facing in four directions) is the balancing force that links Vishnu, the agent of light, and Shiva, lord of darkness, together. Although Brahma is important, there are only two known temples dedicated exclusively to his worship, while both Shiva and Vishnu are worshipped extensively as principal deities.

LEFT Vishnu and his consort, Lakshmi, ride upon Garuda, the eagle who symbolizes the wisdom attained by an open mind.

VISHNU

Also called the Preserver, Vishnu maintains the harmony of the universe and is a manifestation of the sun as it crosses the heavens each day with three great strides, at dawn, noon and sunset. As preserver of the world, he is said to have assumed ten incarnations, referred to as "avatars" (literally "one who descends"); these include Rama, Krishna and the Buddha. As Lord of the Universe, Vishnu floats on the primeval waters, asleep on the serpent Ananta. His four main symbols are the *shanka* (or conch shell), used to dispel demons, the *gaddha* (or club) to represent power, the *chakra* (or discus) used against evil forces, and the *padma* (or lotus) symbolizing reincarnation. *Tulasi* (sweet basil) is sacred to Vishnu and is kept in temples dedicated to him, its leaves used in sacred ceremonies.

SHIVA

A deity of contrasting and often contradictory characteristics, Shiva represents not only destruction, but also regeneration, just as order arises out of chaos, and new life emerges after death. As Nataraja, he is lord of the universal dance of creation and destruction through which he maintains the balance of the cosmos. The dancing Shiva is usually depicted with four hands surrounded by a circle of flames, representing the sun disc and the creation and continuation of the cosmos. Shiva is also the supreme god of masculine virility, symbolized by the phallus-shaped linga (the counterpart of the

female yoni), as well as an ascetic yogi, clad in ashes and animal skins. His third eye (the chakra in the middle of the forehead) can destroy with fire all those who look upon it, while also granting transcendent wisdom. Shiva is sometimes depicted riding the white bull, Nandi, symbol of power and virility, who often appears at shrines to the god.

SHAKTI

The concept of Shakti is another important aspect of the divine. Shakti is the feminine principle, the dynamic life-giving energy of the universe that activates creativity; without Shakti, the other gods remain passive and lacking in motivation. Shakti is often shown embracing Shiva and has two sides to her nature, one gentle and serene, the other fierce and formidable. The goddess Kali, usually shown with a black tongue, rolling eyes, pointed teeth and a garland of skulls, is a personification of the latter, while Parvati, consort of Shiva, represents the former.

THE SOUND OF OM

In Sanskrit calligraphy, the mystic syllable *om* is the symbolic representation of Brahman. It is described in the Upanishads (one of the sacred texts of Hinduism) as the sound that creates and sustains the cosmos, and it is thought that through its utterance, the whole universe (past, present and future) is encapsulated. The sound contains the three sounds of A, U and M, representing the three gods (Brahma, Vishnu and Shiva) who

control life. They also symbolize the three human states of dreaming, sleeping and waking, and the three capacities of desire, knowledge and action. Om is used as a mantra in meditation as well as in sacred ceremony.

DAILY WORSHIP

Puja, or daily worship, is usually carried out in the home and is the main form of Hindu worship, although worship led by a priest also occurs twice a day at the *mandir* (temple). At home, worship is held at a shrine, where the family's chosen deities are represented in the form of pictures or statues, known as *murtis.* At the mandir, a highly ritualized ceremony known as the *arti* takes place. This involves the lighting of five divas by the priest, who circles the lamps in front of the central deity, while the worshippers sing a devotional scriptural verse. At the end of the ceremony, a symbolic offering of food (such as fruit, nuts or sweets) is presented to the deity for blessing and then shared among the congregation.

FESTIVALS

The Hindu year contains many festivals to mark events in the lives of deities or to celebrate the changing seasons. They are lively, colourful affairs involving music, dance and drama and provide an opportunity for families and friends to come together. Held in honour of the goddess Lakshmi, Diwali, the festival of lights, is the most widely celebrated festival in India, symbolizing the triumph of good over evil. In some regions,

RIGHT Diwali (the festival of lights) involves the symbolic offering of light to represent the triumph of good over evil.

Diwali (in October or November) marks the new year; it augurs a fresh start, and is a time when debts are paid, and homes are cleaned, repainted and lit with an array of lights. The festival of Holi, in March, celebrates the grain harvest and is very high-spirited, with bonfires, tricks (such as showering people with coloured dyes) and dancing.

THE GANGES

In a land of heat and dust, the great rivers of India are an important source of life and energy and unsurprisingly are revered as holy. The most important is the Ganges, worshipped as the goddess Ganga, which flows across India from its source in the Himalayas, also held sacred. Pilgrimages are made to Varanasi (associated with Shiva) on the Ganges' banks to wash in the river's sacred waters. It is believed that Ganga offers liberation from *samsara,* the cycle of rebirth, and Varanasi is considered an auspicious site for cremation and for scattering the ashes of the deceased. Pilgrimages are also made to holy sites in the Himalayas, particularly to Mount Kailas, where it is said that Shiva sits in meditation.

ABOVE The Om symbol represents the sacred sound of creation.

BELOW Shiva, dancing in a circle of flames, is a cosmic symbol of life, death and rebirth.

THE COW

In Hinduism, the cow is held sacred, and slaughtering one is considered a terrible crime. Symbols of fertility and plenty, cows are central to Indian agriculture, their milk is an important food source, while oxen are used to pull the plough, allowing the planting of grain.

BUDDHISM

ABOVE When the Buddha cut off his hair he was using the act as a symbol of his decision to renounce the world.

BELOW A Buddha's footprint decorated with Buddhist symbols, including the reversed swastika, an ancient symbol that predates the German Nazis.

Some 2,500 years ago, Siddhartha Gautama, the founder of Buddhism, was born on the border between Nepal and northern India. The Buddha – or Awakened One – is the title he was given after he achieved spiritual self-realization, or "enlightenment", becoming the embodiment of perfect wisdom and compassion. Buddhism is not based on a belief in God, nor does it have a set creed, a central authority, or a universally accepted sacred scripture. Never demanding sole allegiance from its followers, Buddhism has coexisted with local religious traditions and has given us a rich tradition with a diversity of symbols and mythic thinking.

LIFE OF THE BUDDHA

Siddhartha Gautama's life story is fundamental to Buddhism, symbolizing many of its basic teachings, including the need for great effort, complete detachment and boundless compassion. Raised as a prince, Gautama renounced his riches and abandoned his family in search of the cause of life's suffering. After many years as a wandering ascetic, he concluded that neither indulgence nor extreme austerity held the answer and sat down to meditate on the problem under a bodhi tree in the village of Bodhgaya, India. It was here that he became enlightened and experienced nirvana – a blissful state of perfect peace, knowledge and truth. Though no longer bound to the physical world, the Buddha decided, out of compassion, to spend the rest of his life teaching. He gave his first sermon to a small group of disciples at Sarnath, where he taught the Four Noble Truths and the Eightfold Path, teachings which explain the nature of suffering and how to end it. The path involves discipline of thought and action and endorses a way of life that seeks to harm no one. The monastic sangha (assembly) was inaugurated by the Buddha to preserve and spread his teaching.

THE BODHISATTVAS

While some forms of Buddhism focus upon personal salvation, there is also a way to Buddhahood referred to as "the path of the bodhisattva". A bodhisattva is a disciple of Buddhism (either male or female) who is capable of attaining nirvana – and hence freedom from samsara (the rebirth cycle) – but chooses to remain in the physical world in order to help others. In Pali (a language derivative of Sanskrit), the word bodhisattva means "one who is the essence of truth and wisdom". Bodhisattvas are differentiated from the Buddha by their relaxed pose, often depicted seated or lying down to show their continuing relationship with humankind. Among the most important bodhisattvas are Maitreya (Mili in China), a benevolent figure of the future, an awaited messiah of Buddhism, usually shown seated in the Western style; and Avalokiteshvara (Guan-Yin in China), the embodiment of compassion and mercy.

BUDDHIST COSMOLOGY

Unlike the Western view of a cosmos that proceeds from beginning to end, Buddhist cosmology is cyclical. This not only applies to human life (the endless birth, death, rebirth cycle) but also to world systems. These will come into being, pass away and be succeeded by a new order. Some Buddhists also believe that there are countless world systems in existence simultaneously, each having its own Buddha, some of whom have names and can be interacted with. Thus buddha icons do not always represent the historical Buddha Gautama, (also referred to as Shakyamuni Buddha), but may depict buddhas in different incarnations. One such is Amitabha, the Buddha of Infinite Light and guardian of the West, who is often shown holding a lotus flower and accompanied by a peacock.

THE STUPA

One of the most important and easily recognizable symbols of Buddhism is the stupa. In ancient texts, the word stupa meant "summit", and originally stupas were burial mounds containing sacred relics of the Buddha, or else of his main disciples (some of whom also attained enlightenment). As well as being a symbol of the Buddha and his final release from samsara, the stupa is also a cosmic symbol. Although there are many architectural variations, typically it consists of a dome (*anda*), symbolizing both the "world egg" (an archetypal symbol of creation) and the womb, while the relics it houses represent the seeds of life. Usually the dome rests on a square pedestal, which is typically aligned with the four cardinal points, signifying the dome of Heaven resting upon the earth. Stupas later developed into places of worship, and have sometimes been built to commemorate important events.

PRAYER WHEEL

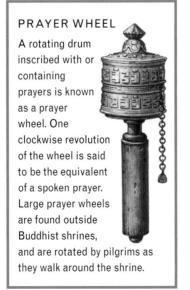

A rotating drum inscribed with or containing prayers is known as a prayer wheel. One clockwise revolution of the wheel is said to be the equivalent of a spoken prayer. Large prayer wheels are found outside Buddhist shrines, and are rotated by pilgrims as they walk around the shrine.

BUDDHA'S FOOTPRINT

In Buddhism (and also Hinduism) footprints can represent the presence of a holy person or deity, encapsulating all their qualities and attributes. Many Buddhist temples contain carvings of copies of the Buddha's footprint, often with auspicious Buddhist symbols such as the eight-spoked wheel, symbolizing the Buddha's law. The Buddha's footprints are also decorated with symbols such as the fish, swastika, diamond mace, conch shell, flower vase and crown. It is thought that if devotees follow in the Buddha's footsteps, they too may attain enlightenment or Buddhahood.

TIBETAN BUDDHISM

Buddhism has tended to adapt itself to the different countries and cultures to which it has spread. Sometimes referred to as the Vajrayana (Diamond or Thunderbolt vehicle), Tibetan Buddhism is characterized by a pantheon of Buddhas and bodhisattvas, and many colourful rituals, artefacts and works of art. The importance of living teachers is stressed; some (known as lamas) are believed to be reincarnations of holy teachers from earlier times, living on earth as bodhisattvas. Ritual practices involve making mandalas (abstract, wheel-like designs), chanting mantras and performing mudras (symbolic hand gestures). Statues and mandalas are used to focus the mind in meditation.

ZEN BUDDHISM

Space and simplicity characterize Zen Buddhism. Developed in China, Korea and Japan, the Zen tradition has influenced Sino-Japanese art forms, such as calligraphy, painting and poetry, as well as the arrangement of flowers and gardens, the tea ceremony, and even martial arts, all of which share order, simplicity and set procedures.

ABOVE A golden Dharma-chakra, an 8-spoked wheel that symbolizes the teachings of the Buddha, stands between two statues of deer, representing the Buddha's first sermon at Deer Park, Sarnath. Jokhang Temple, Lhasa, Tibet.

ABOVE The many-layered symbol for the stupa.

THE ELEPHANT AND THE BUDDHA

The story of the Buddha's birth is surrounded by portents of his greatness. While pregnant, his mother dreamed of giving birth to a white bull-elephant with six tusks. The arrival of a chosen one had long been predicted, and interpreters took this dream as an announcement of his impending arrival. In Indian culture, the white elephant is the mount of Indra, king of the gods, and elephants are called "the removers of obstacles", an attribute given to the Hindu elephant-headed god, Ganesh. In Buddhism the elephant is sometimes used as a symbol of the Buddha, representing his serenity and power.

JUDAISM

ABOVE The eastern wall of every synagogue contains the Torah scrolls, which are read from a raised platform to signify respect. A lamp burns perpetually as a symbol of the Jewish people's covenant with God.

ABOVE The Ark of the Covenant is a symbol of the Exodus.

The world's oldest monotheistic religion, Judaism has a continuity of tradition covering some 4,000 years. The name "Judaism" is derived from the tribe of Judah, one of the twelve tribes of Israel, but it is the life of Abraham – known as the father of the Jewish people – and his relationship with God that is fundamental to Judaism. The Jewish scriptures tell how God made a covenant, or agreement, with Abraham: that his descendants would be God's chosen people, in return for which the people should keep God's laws. These laws were given to Moses on Mount Sinai as he led the Jewish people out of captivity in Egypt (the Exodus) to Canaan (Israel), the land God had promised to Abraham.

THE PROMISED LAND

Judaism's history is rooted in Israel, the promised land. More than just a place, it is one of Judaism's most important symbols, part of the Jewish people's ethnic identity. Jerusalem, city of David, Israel's greatest king, is particularly important. It was here that David's son, Solomon, built a temple, a symbol of communion between man and God. The temple was rebuilt many times until its final destruction by the Roman emperor Titus in AD 70. The Wailing (or Western) Wall is the last remnant of the temple and is a place of pilgrimage and prayer for Jews from all over the world.

THE TORAH

Study of the holy scriptures is one of the most important aspects of the Jewish faith. The first five books of the Hebrew Bible are known as the Pentateuch, or Torah, believed to contain all of God's teaching as revealed to Moses on Mount Sinai.

More than a repository of laws and stories, the Torah is seen as the inner, or spiritual, dimension of the world itself, the medium through which the individual may gain access to higher realms. Every synagogue has a set of parchment scrolls (the Sefer Torah) on which the Torah is handwritten in Hebrew by a specialist scribe; it can take a year to complete. Each scroll has a belt to hold it when rolled, a breastplate and a crown, together with a silver pointer used when reading, to avoid finger contact with the parchment. One of the most sacred symbols of Judaism, the Torah scrolls are kept in a special cupboard or alcove (known as the Holy Ark, after the Ark of the Covenant) in the wall that faces Jerusalem.

THE SYNAGOGUE

After the destruction of the temple, the Jews were scattered throughout the Roman Empire, and the synagogue became the centre of Jewish community life. The synagogue has three main functions: it is a house of

BELOW The *shofar* is a ram's horn trumpet used in Jewish rituals. It recalls the story of Abraham and Isaac and is a sign of God's grace.

JEWISH MYSTICISM

The Torah is said to comprise four levels of meaning: the literal, the allegorical, the homiletical (teaching or preaching) and the secret or mystical. Mystical interpretations view the Torah as a means of understanding the nature of God. The Kabbalah, the most influential strand of Jewish mysticism, conceives of God's attributes as a series of ten spheres (or sephiroth), through which the individual must pass in order to reach the divine source. All aspects of human life are ultimately expressions of the sephiroth, which constitutes the deepest reality, our contact with God. The Kabbalah's central text is the Zohar (Book of Splendour), which was first circulated in Spain in the 13th century. Symbols associated with the Kabbalah include the Star of David and the Tetragrammaton.

RIGHT At Pesach (Passover), the symbolic meal includes bitter herbs and unleavened bread to commemorate slavery in Egypt.

assembly where the Jewish community can meet for any purpose; a house of study, where the scriptures are studied and children learn Hebrew and study the Torah; and a house of prayer, where services are held on the Sabbath (Shabbat). Men and women occupy separate areas, and in obedience to the Second Commandment, there are not usually any images of people or animals. Every synagogue also has a perpetually burning lamp before the Ark – a symbol of God's eternal light, illuminating the darkness of ignorance.

TETRAGRAMMATON

According to tradition, God's name was revealed to Moses, but was so sacred that it could never be spoken aloud. The tetragrammaton comprises the four letters, Y, H, W, H, which spell the true name of God in Hebrew, referred to as "the name" (*ha shem*), or Adonai ("My Lord"). When vowels are added, the letters spell the name Yahweh, which some Christians translate as Jehovah.

The tetragrammaton was engraved on the rod of Aaron and the ring of Solomon, both emblems of authority. The rod was also believed to have miracle-working properties (like the wand, common to many traditions), and Solomon's ring was said to give him powers of divination. In Kabbalism, the tetragrammaton was believed to signify life and to possess magical and healing powers. It is often written on amulets and on plaques displayed in the

synagogue, as well as in Jewish homes, a constant reminder of God's omnipresence.

LAWS AND CUSTOMS

It is said that the law was given to Moses at Mount Sinai on two stones, known as the Tablets of the Decalogue (the Ten Commandments), engraved by the finger of God. At the heart of Jewish belief is the Shema, the first commandment – love of God. The words of the Shema are written on tiny scrolls and placed in small boxes (tefillin), with straps or tapes attached to them. During weekday prayers, Orthodox Jewish males wear the tefillin bound to their foreheads, left arm and hands. Shema scrolls are also put into small boxes called "mezuzah", which are nailed to the doorways of the home (usually outside every room, except the bathroom and toilet), harking back to the time when the words of the Shema were carved into doorposts.

Typically, Orthodox Jewish men wear a small cap (yarmulke) to show their submission to God. The tallit is a fringed garment – usually a cloak or shawl – worn by male Jews. This refers to a passage from Numbers (15:38–39), which instructs that tassels with a blue cord should be attached to undergarments as a reminder of the commandments of God. Orthodox Jewish women are required to cover their hair in the presence of men other than their husband, as a sign that he alone may enjoy their sexuality; most achieve this by wearing a wig in public.

FESTIVALS

Jewish history and teaching is embodied in its festivals, in which traditions are passed on by means of stories, actions, symbolic food, and singing. There are five major festivals, or Days of Awe, laid down in the Torah: Rosh Hashanah (Jewish New Year), Yom Kippur (Day of Atonement), Pesach (Passover), Shavuot (Pentecost) and Sukkoth (the Feast of the Tabernacles), with many symbols connected to each.

Laws governing the consumption of food are a central part of the Jewish faith. During Pesach only unleavened bread (matzah) is eaten, as a reminder of the Exodus, when the Israelites had to leave Egypt in a hurry, with no time to bake ordinary bread. Bitter herbs symbolize slavery in Egypt, and a lamb bone symbolizes the Pesach offerings that would have been brought to the temple in Jerusalem.

The *shofar*, a ram's horn trumpet, is blown during Rosh Hashanah, a call for people to repent and start the new year afresh. This horn is a reminder of God's grace when he allowed Abraham to sacrifice a ram instead of Isaac. There are three main sounds blown on the *shofar*, and during Rosh Hashanah, they are repeated 100 times.

BELOW The Tetragrammaton spells the true name of God in Hebrew, which is never spoken aloud.

STAR OF DAVID

One of the most widely recognized signs of Judaism, today the Star of David is a symbol of the State of Israel, appearing since 1948 on its national flag. A six-pointed star formed from two interlocking triangles, it is said to derive from the hexagrammic shield that David carried against Goliath. The white of the upper triangle and the black of the lower triangle symbolize the union of opposites.

CHRISTIANITY

ABOVE The labarurm, or Chi-Rho cross.

ABOVE Jesus crucified on the cross is a central Christian motif.

ABOVE One of the oldest secret symbols for Christ.

Together with Islam, Christianity is the most widespread of the world's religions. Emerging out of Judaism, it has many different traditions, but its central tenet is that the Jewish-born Jesus of Nazareth is the Son of God, the long-awaited Messiah whose coming was foretold by the Old Testament prophets. The life of Jesus, from his humble birth to the Virgin Mary to his crucifixion, death and resurrection, form the basis of Christian theology as told in the Gospels (meaning "good news") of the New Testament.

SYMBOLS OF CHRIST

Christianity takes its name from the Greek translation of the Hebrew "Messiah" (the Anointed One). Christ is the title Jesus was given by his followers and is symbolized in many ways.

The fish is one of the earliest Christian symbols, found on graves in the Roman catacombs – an ancient, secret meeting place when the Christians were persecuted by the Romans for their faith. It is based on an acrostic: the initial letters of the Greek words for Jesus Christ, Son of God and Saviour spell out ichthus, the Greek word for fish. Christ also referred to his apostles as "fishers of men", while the early Christian fathers called the faithful pisculi (fish).

Another of the earliest symbols for Christ is the labarurm, a monogram composed of the first Greek letters of Christ's name, X (chi) and P (rho). Also known as the Chi-Rho cross, the letters are usually inscribed one over the other, sometimes enclosed within

a circle, becoming both a cosmic and a solar symbol. It is said that the Roman emperor Constantine I had a vision of the Chi-Rho cross promising victory to his army, after which he converted to Christianity. Byzantium, the capital of the Eastern Roman Empire, was renamed Constantinople (Istanbul) and became the centre of the Eastern Orthodox Christian Church.

Other symbols associated with Christ are objects linked to the Passion (or crucifixion). These include the cross on which he died, a crown of thorns, a scourge or whip, the hammer and nails used to fix him to the cross, a spear that the Roman soldiers used to pierce his side, and the ladder by which he was lowered from the cross. From the 14th century, these objects became the

BELOW Jesus the Good Shepherd carries a lamb back to the fold, a symbol of Christ as Saviour.

ABOVE The crown of thorns is a Christian symbol of the crucifixion.

focus of intense devotion among some Christians, designed to arouse an emotional response to Jesus' suffering.

SHEEP AND SHEPHERDS

Jesus drew heavily on his native land and culture for symbols to use in his teachings. For instance, many people in the region would have kept sheep, and the comparison between Jesus as a shepherd and his followers as his flock is a key metaphor.

In John's Gospel, Jesus is referred to as the Good Shepherd who will lead those who have gone astray back to a proper relationship with God, while he is also referred to as "the lamb of God", symbolizing the sacrifice he made, dying in order that humanity's sins may be forgiven. In Christian iconography, Jesus is often shown with a lamb draped over his shoulders, symbolizing his ability to save lost souls. He also carries a shepherd's crook, or crozier, which has been adopted by bishops of the Church and has become a symbol of their pastoral authority over their congregation, as well as a reminder of Jesus.

THE DOVE

In Judaic and Christian cultures, the dove holding an olive branch symbolizes God's grace. As punishment for humanity's wickedness, God had sent a great flood, symbol of destruction and also purification and cleansing. The righteous Noah was warned, and built an ark in which his family and a pair of every animal were saved. After the rain stopped, Noah sent out a dove to search for dry land. It returned, carrying an olive branch from the Mount of Olives, a symbol of God's forgiveness. In Christian iconography the dove is used to represent the Holy Spirit, with seven doves signifying the Holy Spirit's seven gifts.

THE TRINITY

Although Christianity is monotheistic, Christians believe that God shows himself in three different and distinct ways – as Father, Son and Holy Spirit. This threefold nature of God is known as the Trinity. Although each aspect of the Trinity is whole in itself, each is also part of God and the one Godhead. In the 5th century, Saint Patrick used the shamrock, a plant with one stem and three leaves, to try to explain the concept: just as each leaf is distinct, so each is also an integral part of the plant. According to John the Baptist, the Trinity was present at the baptism of Jesus: the Son in the water, the Father speaking words of approval from the heavens, and the Holy Spirit descending to Earth in the form of a dove.

THE VIRGIN MARY

Also known as the Madonna (Italian for "my lady"), the Virgin Mary is honoured as the chosen mother for God's holy son, particularly by the Roman Catholic Church. Mary is represented by a great variety of symbols, including the Madonna lily and white rose, which represent her purity, and the red rose (the Passion of Christ), as well as the sun, moon and a halo of twelve stars, which appear to be linked to the apocalyptic vision described in Revelation (12:1) of a woman "robed with the sun, beneath her feet the moon, and on her head a crown of twelve stars". Other symbols of her sanctity and virginity include an enclosed garden, a closed gate and a mirror. She is usually shown with a halo (a symbol in Christian iconography for divinity and majesty) and wearing a blue cloak, the cloak signifying protection and its colour linking her with the skies and the heavenly realm, as well as with the waters of baptism. The Virgin also became a symbol herself, worshipped as the Divine Mother.

THE CHURCH

Although we use the word "church" to describe a building where Christian worship takes place, strictly speaking it means "group of believers", or those who gather together in the name of Jesus. Traditionally churches are built in the shape of a cross, the universal symbol of Christianity, a reminder of Jesus' death.

THE EUCHARIST

Most churches hold a service known as the Eucharist, also known as Mass or Holy Communion, to commemorate the Last Supper. This is the meal that Jesus shared with his twelve disciples the night before his arrest. Like the Last Supper, the Eucharist involves sharing bread and wine, representations of the flesh and blood of Christ, to symbolize taking Christ's body, or essence, within.

ABOVE An image of the Virgin Mary, showing her with a halo in which there are twelve stars. This picture depicts the immaculate conception, and Mary stands on a crescent moon, a symbol of chastity. She also wears the blue robes that link her with heaven.

THE FOUR EVANGELISTS

The writers of the first four books of the New Testament – Matthew, Mark, Luke and John – are known collectively as the four Evangelists. Apocalyptic visions in the Book of Revelation, as well as those of the Old Testament prophets Daniel and Ezekiel, associate Matthew with an angel, Mark with a lion, Luke with an ox and John with an eagle. In the Western Hermetic tradition, they are linked respectively with the Zodiac signs of Aquarius, Leo, Taurus and Scorpio, the four points of the compass, the four directions and the four elements, as well as the Archangels Raphael, Michael, Gabriel and Uriel.

ISLAM

ABOVE A detail from the Qur'an, the words themselves of which are believed to signify the divine presence.

ABOVE The star and crescent moon symbol is an emblem of the Islamic world.

THE MINARET

The word "minaret" is derived from the Arabic *manara*, meaning "giving off light", alluding perhaps to its symbolic function as a beacon of illumination to the surrounding community. A minaret is a slim tower with a balcony from which the muezzin (caller) calls the faithful to prayer, a constant reminder of Allah's presence. The minaret itself suggests mediation between the people assembled in the mosque below and the heavens above to which it points. The crescent moon, one of the symbols of Islam, is sometimes positioned at the top of the minaret.

The name Islam is from an Arabic word meaning "to submit", with a Muslim being "one who submits" – that is, one who lives in the way intended by Allah (God). As Allah is One, there is no division between the sacred and the secular, with every aspect of life governed by Islamic moral principles. The central tenet of Islam is that it is the original religion, the faith revealed to all the prophets, including Adam, Abraham, Moses and Jesus, but culminating with Mohammed, the last and most important of Allah's divine messengers. Mohammed (or "the Prophet") was born in Makkah, Arabia (now in Saudi Arabia), in the 6th century AD. He is believed to have restored the purity of the teachings of Allah, so bringing Allah's message of guidance to the world to completion and perfection.

FIVE PILLARS OF ISLAM

Islam is built on five main beliefs: belief in Allah, in the Qur'an, in the angels, in Mohammed and the prophets who went before him, and in the Last Day. Muslims also believe that faith alone is meaningless but must be backed up by action in everyday life. These actions are known as "the five pillars of Islam" (a pillar symbolizing support) and are faith, prayer, fasting, pilgrimage and charity.

THE QUR'AN

The sacred text of Islam is known as the Qur'an (derived from the Arab word for "recite"). Muslims believe that this is Allah's own Word, not that of any human being, as directly transmitted to Mohammed over a period of 23 years through the Angel Jibril (Gabriel) in a series of visions. As Mohammed received each portion of the text, he learned it by heart, with Allah teaching him how to recite it.

The actual words of the Qur'an are seen to signify the divine presence of Allah, and so must be written clearly and carefully in the original Arabic; translations are never used in worship. Qur'anic calligraphy has developed as a devotional art, with passages from the Qur'an used to decorate buildings and artefacts – figurative representations are not encouraged in Islam as they are considered tantamount to idolatry. Copies of the Qur'an are always handled with great care, and are kept on a high shelf, wrapped in a clean cloth. A stand is used to hold the book open while reading, and before handling the book, Muslims always make sure that their hands are clean.

THE MOSQUE

Muslims worship Allah in the mosque, or masjid (place of prostration), oriented towards Mecca – with its direction indicated by a mihrab, or niche in the wall. As Islamic sacred art is non-figurative, mosques are decorated with arabesques and geometric patterns, as well as calligraphy from the Qur'an. The patterns reflect the fundamental harmony of the universe and the natural world, derived from the Islamic belief that Allah is One. Although styles of mosque architecture and decoration vary according to local custom and period, many mosques have a domed roof representing the heavenly sky, the universe and creation, usually crowned by a minaret. Other characteristic features include an enclosing courtyard, walkways, and fountains (or showers) for the ablutions required by Islam. Shoes are not worn in the mosque, as they are regarded as unclean. Because Allah is

THE HAND OF FATIMA

Fatima was the daughter of Mohammed and his beloved wife Aisha. Although she is not mentioned in the Qur'an, the Shiite Muslim tradition gives her similar attributes to the Virgin Mary, referring to her as the "Mistress of the Women of the Worlds", the "Virgin" and the "Pure and Holy", and says that she was created from the light of Allah's greatness, or from the food of paradise. In popular religion, the faithful rely on Fatima, who takes the part of the oppressed in the struggle against injustice begun by her father. Shiite women travel to shrines dedicated to Fatima, where they pray for her help with their problems. Amulets known as "the hand of Fatima" are sacred and are worn for protection. The five fingers of the hand also symbolize the five pillars of Islam.

ANGELS

In Islam, angels are creatures of light who praise Allah and carry out his instructions. Jibril, chief of the angels, was responsible for bringing Allah's guidance to all the prophets, including Mohammed. Angels pray for human beings, especially believers, and support the faithful. Muslims believe that everyone has two angels whose task is to record that person's deeds for the Last Day.

everywhere, Islam teaches that the whole world is a mosque, so that the mosque itself can be thought of as a world symbol. The mosque is also regarded as a centre for education, and some of the great mosques of history have had schools and libraries attached to them.

RITUALS AND CUSTOMS

Mohammed decreed that "Cleanliness is part of faith", so before *salah* (prayer), worshippers must wash. This ritual cleansing, or *wadu*, is a symbolic act, the water not only washing the physical body but also cleansing the soul from sin. If water is unavailable, dry ablution using dust or sand is permissible.

In communal worship, Muslims stand side by side, symbolizing the equality of all in Allah's eyes. Men and women are separate, however, and the Iman, who leads the prayers, is in front. Parts of the Qur'an are recited, followed by a series of formal actions that include bowing and prostrating, (signs of submission to Allah). Special mats are used for prayer, and they are always rolled, not folded, after use.

Fasting plays an important part in Islam, and involves abstaining from food, drink and sex during the daytime. Muslims believe that

fasting increases their awareness that they are always in Allah's presence, and many Muslims fast regularly on certain days all the year round. It is, however, essential for the whole month of Ramadan, the ninth month of the (lunar) Muslim calendar, which commemorates the time when the first words of the Qur'an were revealed to Mohammed. The end of Ramadan is marked by the new moon, when Muslims break their fast with a family feast.

PILGRIMAGE

Every year, millions of Muslims make their pilgrimage (*hajj*) to Mecca, Islam's holy city, a place so sacred that non-Muslims are not allowed to enter. The pilgrims stay in a huge encampment, and before entering the city, they set aside their normal clothes and put on a simple white garment, a sign of equality with others and humility before Allah.

When in Mecca, they pay homage to Islam's most holy structure, the Ka'aba (cube), the central focus of Muslim worship throughout the world. Standing in the courtyard of the Great Mosque in Makkah, the Ka'aba is a simple cube-shaped stone building that, according to tradition, is the first ever house built for the worship of Allah,

rebuilt by Abraham and his son Ishmael. The Ka'aba symbolizes Allah's presence and is covered by a black velvet cloth called the *kiswah*, which is replaced each year. The cloth is a sign of humility and respect, because to gaze on the Ka'aba directly would be akin to looking at Allah, which is forbidden. It is embroidered in gold with passages from the Qur'an, especially on the part over the door – leading to the sacred interior. Reciting prayers, the pilgrims circle the Ka'aba seven times (a mystical number). Walking anticlockwise, they begin at the corner where the sacred Black Stone is embedded in a silver frame. The stone is believed to be a meteorite, a symbol of divine grace and power fallen from Heaven.

BELOW The Ka'aba in the courtyard of the Great Mosque at Mecca is one of Islam's most sacred and profound symbols.

Symbols and the Mind

Modern Western theories about the meaning and use of symbols have been greatly influenced by psychology, the scientific study of the human mind. Symbolism in dreams has been a subject of fascination since ancient times, but in the 19th century pioneering psychologists began to explore its use as a psychoanalytic tool.

Freud and Jung

ABOVE Sigmund Freud believed that symbols are products of the unconscious mind and can contain meaningful information.

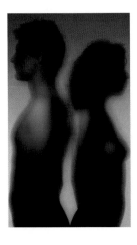

ABOVE According to Jung, male and female are also psychological states, known as the *animus* and *anima*.

Sigmund Freud (1856–1939), who is often referred to as the "father of psychoanalysis", differentiated between the conscious and unconscious mind. His seminal work, *The Interpretation of Dreams* (1900), postulates that symbols are a product of the unconscious, typically produced while in the dreaming state as a way of communicating with the conscious self, or ego. A one-time pupil of Freud's, Carl Gustav Jung (1875–1961) broke away from his mentor, developing his theory of the "collective unconscious", a mythical level of the unconscious whose symbolism is archetypal rather than personal.

EROS AND THANATOS

Freud identified two coinciding and conflicting instinctual drives: *eros* and *thanatos*. Eros, or sexuality, is the drive of life, love and creativity; thanatos, or death, is the drive of aggression and destruction. The struggle between them is central to human life, with neuroses occurring when instinctual urges are denied (because they are painful or anti-social) and repressed in the unconscious mind. As products of the unconscious, symbols are a way of finding out more about these repressions.

SEXUAL SYMBOLISM

Put simply, anything that is erect or can penetrate, or resembles a phallus in any way, is a symbol of male sexuality. Freud remarks: "All elongated objects, such as sticks, tree trunks and umbrellas (the opening of these last being comparable to an erection), may stand for the male organ." Other examples could include mountains, tall buildings, trains, pens or bananas. Conversely, anything that can be entered, that is concealed, or resembles the vulva and/or vagina in any way is a symbol of female sexuality: for instance, valleys, caves, doorways, boxes, drawers, cupboards, fruit such as figs, or flowers such as roses. Female breasts are suggested by curving or round shapes, for instance domed buildings, rolling hills or any round fruit such as gourds or melons. However, Freud himself recognized that such things are not inevitably sexual symbols, and is reputed to have said: "Sometimes a cigar is just a cigar."

ANIMA AND ANIMUS

For Jung, male and female sexuality were expressions of deeper creative forces, referred to by him as the "animus" and "anima". The animus represents the male, or rational, side of the

psyche and the anima the female, intuitive, side; the way they are symbolized varies. If one or the other is repressed, it can become destructive: a "negative animus" could lead to a rigid, controlled or controlling personality. It could also be experienced symbolically in dreams as a threatening male figure, or in waking life as fear of a male authority figure.

COMPENSATION

Jung saw the psyche as self-adjusting: trying to compensate for areas that are out of balance to reconcile its opposing parts. When these are reconciled we are psychologically balanced and

---

SYMBOLIC STRUCTURES

Freud thought of the mind as having three conflicting internal tendencies: the *id* is the unconscious, seat of instinct and desire, the *ego* is the conscious self and the *superego* is an internalized self-critic. To avoid censorship by the superego, the id uses symbolic imagery to communicate with the ego. For Jung, the mind also has three main parts: the conscious mind; the personal unconscious, a storehouse of individual "memories"; and the collective unconscious.

LEFT From a Freudian perspective, the soft rolling contours of a hilly landscape can symbolize the curvy shape of the female form.

ABOVE Carl Jung developed the theory of the collective unconscious, a layer of the mind that uses symbols to express universal human themes.

achieve a state of wholeness. He believed symbols could be used to explore the boundaries between oppositions, and in his clinical work he analyzed the symbols in his patients' dreams, seeing them as clues to their state of mind and indicators of their rate of progress.

THE LIFE PROCESS

Organic growth is fundamental to Jung's thinking, with the human organism designed to develop to psychological as well as physical

BELOW An atomic explosion symbolizes Freud's concept of *thanatos*, or the death wish.

maturity. Jung referred to this as "the process of individuation", with the symbols arising from the unconscious providing clues to the individual's current stage of mental and emotional development. This process is not something that can be brought about by conscious willpower, but just as a seed grows into a plant, is something that happens involuntarily, according to a predetermined pattern. Jung also believed that there was an organizing intelligence in each person's psychic system, the inventor and source of symbols. He referred to this as the Self, and saw it as both the nucleus and the totality of the psyche. Other cultures have also expressed an awareness of an inner centre: for instance, the Greeks referred to it as a *daimon*.

SIGNS AND SYMBOLS

Jung differentiated between signs and symbols, saying that a sign was always linked to the

conscious thought behind it, and by implication was always less than the concept it represented. Symbols, on the other hand, always stood for more than their obvious and immediate meaning, hinting at something not yet known. He thought they were produced spontaneously in the unconscious, and were not something that could be created by conscious intent. He believed they occurred not only in dreams, but in all kinds of psychic manifestations, saying that thoughts and feelings, acts and situations can all be symbolic. He went so far as to say that even inanimate objects can appear to "cooperate" with the unconscious in the arrangement of symbolic patterns, citing examples of well-authenticated stories of clocks stopping, pictures falling, or mirrors shattering at the moment of their owner's death.

A MULTI-STOREYED HOUSE

Jung frequently used the symbols generated by his own dreams to further his understanding of the psyche. For instance, he referred to his dream of exploring a house with several floors to describe the layers of the mind.

The dream began in a first-floor (US second-floor) room, a pleasant sitting room from the 18th century; the surroundings felt comfortable and reasonably familiar. On the ground (US first) floor, the rooms became darker and the furnishings much older, dating back to the 16th century or before. Becoming curious about what was in the rest of the house, he came upon a heavy door. Opening it, he went down to the cellar and found himself in a beautifully vaulted room that looked very ancient. Feeling very excited, he saw an iron ring on a stone slab and pulled it. Beneath the slab was a flight of stairs leading down to a cave, which seemed like a prehistoric tomb, containing skulls, bones and shards of pottery.

Jung thought the first floor related to his conscious self, the ground floor to the personal unconscious, the cellar to the collective unconscious, and the cave to the most primitive layer of the unconscious, bordering on the "animal soul".

ARCHETYPAL SYMBOLS

ABOVE Batman's heroism arises from his ability to integrate his "bat" or Shadow nature with his human nature.

BELOW Sir Galahad, from Arthurian legend, represents the ability to be true to our inner nature, thus fulfilling the Holy Grail quest.

The belief that there are patterns or tendencies organizing nature and human experience has been commonly held throughout human history and across world cultures. The pagan notion of *wyrd* as a preordained web of fate, the Aboriginal Dreaming, and every other mythological system, pantheon of gods or single deity presupposes the idea of an unseen influence behind everyday life. Carl Jung took this principle and developed a psychological theory of deep organizing patterns, or archetypes, shedding light on the shared source of symbolism throughout the world.

THE COLLECTIVE UNCONSCIOUS

Contrary to Freud, Jung believed that the symbols produced by the unconscious did not relate to personal material only. He noted a recurrence of certain symbolic imagery, and a similarity between many of the images he found and the symbols that appear in myth, religion and art, and esoteric traditions such as alchemy. Jung argued that symbolism plays an important role in the psychic processes that influence human life, containing information about human emotions and expressing profound spiritual truths.

JUNG'S ARCHETYPES

An archetype is a basic underlying pattern that gives an event symbolic meaning. Archetypes are not exactly motifs or symbols themselves, but are rather the deep-rooted tendencies or trends that influence symbol formation. Jung understood archetypal images to be grounded in the biology of the body and its organs, connecting us to our evolutionary history and our animal natures. He gave them names such as Anima, Animus, Self, Eros, Mother and Shadow.

Jung considered archetypes, operating at the level of the collective unconscious, to be common to all humanity, beyond the diversities of race, place or history, though the symbolism that arises from archetypal patterns varies: the anima and animus, for example, may appear as fairies and elves or gods and goddesses that are specific to each tradition or mythology.

Archetypes help us to understand common human experiences, such as birth, death, change or transformation, wholeness, growth and development, achievement or failure, wisdom and love.

THE SELF

Jung defined the wholeness for which all humans strive as the Self; it is often symbolized by the circle or the square. The Self is the goal of the individuation process, through which we become our true selves.

The quest for the Holy Grail, in Arthurian legend, can be seen as representing the Self: Sir Galahad finds the Grail and ascends to heaven, or fulfilment of his true nature. The symbol of the car or chariot commonly represents the journey to the Self, demonstrating where a person is on their life path in relation to their wholeness. A house can represent the structure of the Self, and other symbols of the Self include the hero and the mountain.

THE SHADOW

Aspects of a person's nature that are unconscious or not integrated, and which they regard as inferior or bad, are represented by the archetype described by Jung as the Shadow. They include unacceptable desires, undeveloped feelings or ideas, and animal instincts. Lived unconsciously, the Shadow appears as bad or evil figures in dreams or myths. In a dream, the Shadow might appear as a burglar of the same sex as the dreamer. In cultures with restrictive social

codes, the Shadow compensates through becoming more prominent. Vampires are an image of the Shadow. Having a human appearance, they live in the darkness, with hidden desires, feeding on the blood of the living, and drawing power from what we call "normality".

THE MOTHER

Nurturing and protection are embodied in the Mother archetype. She gives life energy to her children, friends and community, and is also associated with reproduction and abundant growth in nature. The negative mother is domineering, interfering, jealous, and may take or destroy life. Some Jungians argue that a woman who is strongly connected with the Mother archetype must learn to nurture herself and her own creative life-force, in order to avoid becoming destructive.

The Mother archetype is found in goddesses of the earth and sky and other Great Mother figures. The Egyptian sky goddess, Nut, is a figure of overarching maternal protection. The Greek earth goddess Demeter (Roman Ceres) is associated with both motherhood and the harvest, and her principal symbols are barley and corn, crops essential to life. The maternal aspect of Mary is found in her manifestation as Queen of Earth.

The destructive aspect of the Mother archetype is more obvious in the Hindu goddess Kali, who is a destroyer but also a mother goddess of creation and protection. Witches in dreams

and fairy tales can also represent the negative aspect of the archetypal Mother. A witch may personify a jealous attitude that resists another person changing or developing for the better. She casts spells on people to hypnotize them, send them to sleep or trap them in a certain place, thus maintaining control. We may dream of witches at a time of transition, when it is hard to leave a certain way of life or belief system.

THE TRICKSTER

Wisdom within foolishness is represented by the archetype of the Trickster. He does not conform to the laws of the everyday world, and challenges authority. Clown figures are common to most cultures throughout the world. In Shakespearean drama, the fool, or court jester, is a recurring character, whose riddles and humour counterbalance the rigid authority of the ruler, indirectly offering him wisdom.

In Nigerian mythology, Edshu was a trickster god who took great delight in provoking arguments among members of a community. He would wear a hat that was red on one side and blue on the other, so that the people would argue about what colour hat he had on. Thus, while appearing to have a destructive effect, through his mischief he helped people to see that there was more than one way of looking at things.

TIMESPIRITS

The contemporary therapist Dr Arnold Mindell has used the word "timespirit" to describe the concept of archetypal roles and relationships that are not static but evolving. It presupposes that we live in a kind of field, like a magnetic field, which both organizes our experience and is influenced by our actions.

Mindell envisages an archetypal or mythical stream flowing through the world, whose flow and direction changes over time. Particular roles that are relevant to a culture, region and history arise, make themselves known within everyday life, then fall away. We are said to be immersed in this stream, and at one time or another we are carried by particular roles or spirits, which touch us personally but are also part of the greater stream.

The concept formalized in such theories, of dreamlike or mythical patterns underlying everyday life experience, suggests that symbolic processes are calling on us to be lived consciously and with awareness. One way of understanding this is that behind every human conflict there are mythical stories trying to unfold.

THE ELDER AS A TIMESPIRIT

The figure of the elder is important in most cultures. As wise figures with an overview for their community or world, elders embody the principle of appreciating and valuing all viewpoints and perspectives. The timespirit of the elder often appears when people need help, but elders are not infallible and they sometimes become stuck or rigid, focusing on the use of power, rules and morality. The United Nations is a symbolic "circle of elders" whose aim is to help in conflict zones.

PROCESS-ORIENTED PSYCHOLOGY

ABOVE An explosion occurring at the edge of awareness in a dream or in "explosive" physical symptoms may signify the need to be more emotionally expressive.

BELOW RIGHT Edges occur in nature where two environments meet. Psychological "edges" are where we meet the limit of what we know or believe we can understand.

BELOW A dream of mist or fog represents the obscuring of our usual perceptions, thus forcing us to use different senses to experience the world.

In the 1960s the psychological theorist and therapist Arnold Mindell founded dreambody work, later renamed Process Oriented Psychology or Process Work. Mindell found common ground in the theory and wisdom of quantum physics, Jungian psychology, shamanism and Taoism, together with other sociological and psychological approaches. Process work is a phenomenological approach, which seeks to increase people's awareness of the pattern, nature and flow of what they experience.

Process work contributes to the study of signs and symbols because it approaches even the most extreme or chaotic events on the basis that they are rooted in archetypal patterns. Bodily symptoms, difficult mental states, life transitions and relationship or global conflicts can all be understood as archetypal and symbolic manifestations, seeking to be unfolded and consciously lived through us in our day-to-day experiences.

PROCESS VERSUS STATES

Mindell points out that we have a tendency to view life in terms of states – fixed symbols, fixed meanings, fixed identities, states of mind – whereas we really live in a world of process – receiving a constant flow of signals and information. He makes the analogy of the process of life as being like a track along which a train moves, with stations representing temporary states. In process work symbols are seen not only as having fixed meanings, but also as being part of an ongoing fluid development requiring constant awareness.

Jung argued that some symbols have a fixed meaning, being archetypes that go beyond cultural and temporal differences. In process work the therapist is guided by a person's feedback to an interpretation rather than by the interpretation itself.

FEEDBACK AND SYMBOL INTERPRETATION

A central concept in process work, which is also inherent in Taoism and many other nature-oriented traditions, is that it is led by feedback. While a symbol can be interpreted by an expert or a professional, the best interpretations are mirrored and confirmed by the signals and responses of the inquirer.

Positive feedback is information that points or leads the way in a person's process. When a dream symbol is interpreted by the therapist, positive feedback may or may not be the verbal response to the interpretation, but can also be found in other signals and responses, such as unconscious movements, feelings or sensations, visual experiences or unintentional sounds.

PRIMARY AND SECONDARY PROCESS

From a process perspective, we might think of symbols as snapshots in a given time and place. Primary symbols are familiar things with which we identify. For example, the badges and uniforms worn by police officers, firefighters or doctors symbolize their identity with their role and professional body, and are primary symbols for them. The national flags and anthems of athletes at the Olympic Games are also primary symbols. When people are asleep, their primary process or identity will appear in dreams as symbolic figures that are familiar or known to them, or as aspects of their past. The dreamer will speak of recognizing

or knowing these figures easily. During the daytime, the primary process is found in the roles, body language, ways of behaving and any other signals close to a person's identity.

Secondary symbolism may inspire or disturb us: it represents aspects of ourselves with which we do not so easily identify, but points to our deeper process and evolution. A secondary process disturbs a person's personal identity, and is experienced as something "other". For example, when a group of people make jokes about another group, the qualities that they are ridiculing may be projected secondary qualities of the jokers themselves.

Secondary symbols in dreams are those symbols with which we are unfamiliar: the bears, gurus, leaders, mysterious flowers, shadowy figures, enemies, attackers and lovers in our dream world. Dreaming of a caged bear, for example, may represent a bearlike aspect of a person's identity – possibly rage, power or a connection with the earth – which has become locked away. Secondary information of this kind might appear in the daytime as a mood of depression, or as tension in the body. Secondary symbolism is commonly projected on to the "enemy" or, conversely, on to people whom we admire.

THE EDGE
Mindell defines the border between our primary identity and secondary processes as the "edge". The edge defines the limits of who we think we are. It is defined by the conscious or unconscious

beliefs we hold about ourselves, and fixes or colours our viewpoint and perspective.

The edge is our growing boundary and psychic "skin". Whenever we are confronted by the unknown, or something that disturbs our view of the world, then we are at an edge. Edge symbols are common in mythology, folklore and dreams.

The forest edge is the line between safety and terror, the conscious and the unconscious, and the human realms and nature. It is where we leave the known for the unknown. Like the forest, the edge between day and night represents that between the light of the conscious and the darkness of the unconscious, though it is a cyclical edge that recurs rhythmically. Many cultures regard the twilight hours or dusk, as a liminal (or transitional) time in which we are closest to the spirits of the dead, or as the time when fairies come out to play. Conversely, dawn symbolizes joy and awakening, a fresh perspective on things.

The cliff edge has connotations of fear and doom, but is simultaneously a symbol of abandon and exhilaration. Seen from the sea, cliffs can be a symbol of hope for the returning traveller and strength against enemies, but they are also places of suicide. The most significant edge of all is that between life and death, often represented by the grave. As a metaphor, death can symbolize a dead end, or a loss of joy or hope, but can also mean a transformation, or transition to a new level in life.

HOW DREAM FIGURES COMMUNICATE
When we consider our bodies as dreaming entities, it seems reasonable that the figures we dream about at night should also be expressed in our bodies during the day. For example, a man was identified with flexibility and an easy-going attitude, and he concentrated a great deal upon relaxing his body. However, he found to his surprise that people related to something intense and unyielding in his personality, communicated through his body posture. He became disturbed by tensions and a sense of rigidity in his posture, and developed headaches that felt like a helmet covering his head. With a slight shift of emphasis upon these symptoms, and by slightly amplifying the tensions within them, he found he stood and walked like a knight in black armour. He had discovered that he was too flexible and needed to stand up for his inner standards.

Process work invites us to revise our fixed approach to life and symbolic meaning, developing instead an awareness that we are part of the flow in a symbolic universe.

ABOVE Figures such as the "black knight" appear symbolically in dreams, and their characteristics may be reflected in our physical symptoms when we are awake.

SYMPTOMS
Mindell's original interest in the relationship between dream symbolism and the information held or channelled through the body led him to work with a man who had a large stomach tumour. Amplifying the experience in his tumour, the man felt that he was going to explode. He was supported to go further, and upon "exploding" found himself expressing feelings that he had held back for years. Afterwards he recalled that he had recently dreamed of a bomb exploding in the centre of the city where he lived.

THE SYMBOLIC LIFE PATH

ECOLOGICAL SELF

The philosopher Arne Naess introduced the idea of the ecological self, through which people realize their deep identification with nature. The eco-logical self is known to many cultures that maintain a close con-nection to the natural world. A Navajo chant goes: "The mountains, I become part of it ... The herbs, the fire tree, I become part of it ..." The aboriginal people, through initia-tion, experience a fun-damental identifica-tion with the land, seeing this not as symbolic, but as a basic reality.

How do we find our way in life? What makes a life path meaningful or fulfilling? Comparative mythologist Joseph Campbell used to tell his students to "follow your bliss", believing this to be the best way to discover an individual's true path. Mythology and symbolism from many cultures present life as a heroic journey, representing a path of self-realization through developing an awareness of, and a connection to, ourselves and the world around us.

THE HERO'S JOURNEY

Within the archetypal journey of the hero, symbolism concerns the human struggle to find identity and a sense of meaning and purpose. The heroic cycle can be described in three distinct parts: the call to adventure, initiation and the return.

At the beginning of the quest a calling invites the hero to cross a physical or psychological threshold and enter the unknown or realm of the unconscious. In the ancient Sumerian epic, the restless king Gilgamesh was called to adventure through meeting his helper Enkidu, eventually travelling through Iran to a forest to fight the demon Humbaba. In Homer's *Odyssey*, Odysseus was held captive on the island of Ogyia, perpetually resisting the nymph Calypso, who tried to win his heart. The god Hermes, messenger of Zeus, finally told Calypso to set him free, whereupon his quest began. King Arthur, with the help of Merlin, began his journey through his unique ability to draw a sword from a stone.

GUARDIANS

Helpers or guardian figures embody the qualities necessary to undertake a heroic journey. The hero is often initially weak or inexperienced, but gains the support of a guardian, who may be an older, wiser figure, an animal helper or a divinity.

In psychological terms, guardian figures symbolize the whole psyche of the individual. Mentors and guardians embody qualities such as love, trust, protection, faith, courage, power and magic. The Navajo guardian spirit, Spider Woman, protected the Twin-Warriors during their journey to the sun, the house of their father. She provided them with a protective hoop with eagle feathers to keep enemies at bay. The young Maori hero Hatupatu, who had been treated badly by his brothers and then murdered by them, was brought back to life by an *atua*, or supernatural being, in the form of a blowfly, sent by his parents.

THRESHOLDS

The heroic journey always involves crossing a threshold between civilization, or the known world, and the wilderness, or the unknown. In Stanley Kubrick's film *2001: A Space Odyssey*, the threshold is crossed by entering space, while for Homer's Odysseus it was sea travel. In the old sagas and heroic tales, the sea was portrayed as the vast unknown, full of mystery. In modern times, space has become the new symbol of the uncharted, unknown territory. In the *Star Trek* adventures, the captain's log referred to space as the "final frontier" in which the Enterprise was to seek out new civilizations, travelling "where no man has gone before".

INITIATION AND TESTS

Crossing the threshold implies being confronted by new challenges that are beyond everyday existence. This is the purpose of initiation in many cultures, through which individuals or groups are caused to extend their identities. Once the hero has embarked on his journey, a variety of powerful adversaries or initiatory tests are faced, involving all manner of challenges, battles and seductions, awakening the hero to his powers and weaknesses. Each heroic victory is truly a victory over the hero's own failings.

In Jungian terms, the Shadow, which embodies disavowed personal qualities such as egotism, laziness, pride, cowardice, possessiveness, jealousy and ambitiousness, must

be confronted and conquered, or accepted and integrated. This may mean fighting an enemy figure, or being presented with some other challenge. One of the labours given to Heracles (Hercules) is to clean up, in one day, decades of dung deposited by hundreds of cattle in the Augean Stables, thus transforming a dirty place (or an undesirable part of himself) into something acceptable.

Heroic battles often involve the hero putting his or her life on the line for another person or ideal. The souls of the Aztec heroes were thought to be assigned to various heavens, depending on the kind of heroism they had shown. This would apply equally to warriors who died in battle and to women who died during childbirth. Many heroes have slain dragons to save damsels in distress, symbolically freeing or protecting their anima, or feminine aspect, from the ravages of jealousy or power.

In the late medieval story of *Don Quixote*, the knight rode out to fight giants, but instead met windmills, contemporary symbols of the new mechanistic world view that had replaced the monsters of old. Increasingly, modern heroes are required to wrestle with technologically advanced adversaries, symbols of our mechanistic nature.

The hero is often challenged with seduction or offers of power, or is held under a spell or trance. In the Arthurian story of *Gawain and the Green Knight*, Sir Gawain must resist the advances of the Green Knight's wife, Bercilak, to prove himself a true knight.

Gawain's hunting of the innocent deer, the wild boar and the cunning fox – each representing one of the qualities used by Bercilak in her attempts to seduce him – depicts his refusal to succumb to her enticements.

Heroes are commonly spellbound by witches, fairies and daemon lovers who try to overcome their willpower, or put them to sleep. Odysseus made his crew fill their ears with wax in order to save themselves from the seductive singing of the alluring Sirens. He himself could not bear to forgo the pleasure of hearing them, but ordered his sailors to tie him to the mast, to prevent him leaping on to the rocks.

The hero must often also journey beyond life into the realms of death. In the Sumerian legend of Inanna the sky goddess, she goes down to the underworld, experiencing death, in order to bring her lover back to life. Jonah, in the Old Testament, is taken into the belly of a whale and is later reborn with new powers. Many totemic cultures depict a tribal leader being eaten by a totem animal, thus becoming one with the animal.

Whatever the trial, the true qualities of the hero are brought out through these encounters during the heroic journey. Each adversary that presents itelf is a symbolic facet of the hero's wholeness, awaiting transformation and integration.

THE RETURN
Once the hero has realized the aims of the quest, he or she can return with a boon or vision for

the benefit of the community. This may be a great treasure hidden in a cave and guarded by a sleeping dragon. It might be a priceless commodity, such as the fire that Prometheus stole from the gods to make human life bearable. The treasures of the unconscious are rarely released until one has developed the ability to face one's deep fears.

Some heroes must be reconciled with their father, marking the point when they can take up their role in society. Some, having integrated all the experiences of the quest, achieve apotheosis – becoming a god. The hero now straddles the worlds of everyday reality and of the gods. Gilgamesh is tricked out of the secret of immortality, but returns home with the wisdom of his own mortality, and the ability to live and enjoy life.

ABOVE The heroic Prometheus bringing his gift of fire to humanity.

BELOW Don Quixote had an impulsive personality, and was determined to live his days fully as if he were about to die.

DREAM SYMBOLISM

ABOVE Amplifying the symbols in your dreams could have an impact on your waking life.

BELOW The archetypal figure of the witch can symbolize feminine power for good or evil.

According to Jung, the totality of a person's dream life represents their potential for individuation. As we respond to our personal world of symbolism, we travel along a path that leads to self-realization, or the Self, Jung's archetype of wholeness.

THE LIFE-MYTH
The Self has parallels in the inner *daimon* of the Greeks, the *genius* of the Romans and the ancient Egyptians' Ka (the spirit or life-force that was created with an individual, and reunited with them at death); in more primitive cultures the idea of a guiding or accompanying spirit is seen in the totemic animals and plants that protect members of a clan. The Naskapi Indians, from the Labrador peninsula, believe their soul is an inner companion called Mista'peo (or "Great Man"), who resides in their heart and after death is thought to reincarnate in another being. They find their way in life by following guidance given to them in dreams.

Childhood dreams are said to contain patterns that are symbolic of our life-myth or path. They commonly portray the everyday personality being threatened and overwhelmed by a powerful mythical figure such as a witch, a Yeti, or a wave, representing aspects of our wholeness that will be met during the course of our lives. For example, a girl may suffer frightening dreams in which she is pursued by a witch, but encouraging her to play at being a witch herself may help her conquer her fears by finding new feminine powers of her own.

The life-myth is the fundamental pattern, or mythic potential, that informs and organizes a person's life path. Dr Arnold Mindell refers to this mythic potential as the "Big You", which underpins the twists and turns of our lives. Every difficulty in life, such as a relationship break-up, chronic physical symptoms, addiction or the loss of a role or identity, would therefore be connected to the life

myth. The challenge to the everyday self, or "Little You", is to take the heroic challenge and wrestle with the Big You until it becomes an ally and will give up its secrets.

AMPLIFICATION TECHNIQUES
A great deal of focus has been given to the interpretation of signs and symbols according to our rational understanding and knowledge of their meaning. But, approached more holistically, it becomes evident that a deeper understanding of the signs and symbols of the psyche will involve not only our minds but also the wisdom of our bodies and nature. Amplification refers to focusing on symbolic content, whether in dreams, the imagination, in our bodies or in nature, and strengthening the experience so that it can unfold, allowing its wisdom to flower.

JUNG'S ACTIVE IMAGINATION
Active imagination is a psychological tool that can help towards achieving wholeness or individuation. It involves direct contact or confrontation with the unconscious, without the need for tests and interpretations.

When a patient is in analysis, the first stage involves some degree of "symbol transference", in which the patient unconsciously transfers symbolic content on to the therapist, who holds these projections until the patient is ready to integrate them. For example, the therapist may represent a negative or positive

mother, father or authority figure for the patient; through the therapeutic relationship, the patient can learn to integrate the qualities that have been projected.

Jung once said that stepping into dreams and using active imagination is the essential second half of analysis, and that without active imagination one could never become truly independent of a psychotherapist.

The basic approach of active imagination is to sit down alone as free as possible from disturbance, concentrating on whatever comes from the unconscious. Often an image or sound will arise in this situation, which must then be prevented from sinking back into the unconscious: this may be achieved by representing it in drawing or painting, writing it down, or possibly expressing it in movement or dance.

A more indirect approach to active imagination is to write stories about another person; this process inevitably brings the storyteller's unconscious into play. Jung also spoke of having conversations with the personified voices of the unconscious, as a later stage of active imagination. At a time when he was in a particularly low point in his life, and was feeling depressed, Jung said he had long and deep conversations with a wise inner figure called Philemon, from whom he felt he had received great insights.

Jung viewed active imagination in many respects as replacing the importance of dreaming, in that it was a direct contact with, and

ABOVE The dreams of young adults and children, whether benign or malign, are believed to contain patterns that symbolize our life path.

amplification and expression of, the archetypes. In his latter years, Jung spent a great deal of time engaged in active imagination, playing in the sand and carving stone sculptures at his home in Böllingen, Switzerland.

PROCESS AMPLIFICATION

Inspired by Jung's approaches to amplification, Dr Arnold Mindell developed a more explicit approach to amplifying dreamlike information as it occurs in different channels of perception.

As individuals we have preferred, or "occupied", channels of perception (or senses), and less preferred, or "unoccupied", channels. Some people think and perceive physical sensations primarily in pictures, while others interpret the world in words. If a person tends to perceive the world through vision or through sound and words, then they have occupied visual or auditory channels. A person who naturally favours "feeling" or movement is said to occupy the proprioceptive or kinaesthetic channels of perception. In each case other

channels will be relatively unoccupied. The information that does occupy these channels tends to disturb us, and yet at the same time it can have meaningful symbolic content, pointing to less-known aspects of ourselves.

THE SENOI TEMIARS

For some cultures, the amplification of dream symbols is second nature. The Senoi Temiars of northern Malaysia place great value upon dream-life, and the exploration and expression of this dream-life is used to further the social life and projects of the community. They use a playful form of trance dance and community singing in order to connect with and amplify dream material.

The Senoi Temiars also encourage the telling of dreams at breakfast time, and if a child is fearful of a dream, for example a dream in which they are falling, the parents will help the child to learn to dream lucidly, so that they can control the course of the dream – they can then change the uncontrolled falling into controlled flight.

THE JEWEL IN THE WOUND

Rose-Emily Rothenberg used active imagination to work with a serious skin disorder that she had had from childhood. She described how she remodelled herself through creative play. Initially she viewed the scars on her body as an inferior part of her, which she wished to have removed, however, over time she began to relate to the scars as "stars" or jewels, guides to parts of her that she felt were out of control and in pain.

SYMBOLS IN SYNCHRONICITY

FAR RIGHT A clock stopping at the moment of its owner's death is a good example of synchronicity. The theory of synchronicity uses symbols to relate the meaning of two otherwise disparate events, thus creating a "meaningful coincidence".

Jung coined the term "synchronicity" to describe coincidences of two or more events that he felt could not be due to chance alone. In his 1952 book *Synchronicity: an Acausal Connecting Principle*, he expounded his theory that this kind of "meaningful coincidence of inner and outer experience" was not governed by the principle of causality, but was a case of internal psychic states influencing external events. The concept has been used to explain otherwise unaccountable phenomena such as telepathy, astrology and the interpretation of the Tarot.

In cases of synchronicity, seemingly unrelated things are found to have a connection because, in Jung's view, they share the common ground of the *unus mundus*, or "one world", the mythical dimension behind all life. Such events carry meaningful symbols across the threshold between the unconscious and the conscious.

COINCIDENCES AT THE SAME TIME AND PLACE

Jung famously recounted one of his own experiences of synchronicity, in which a patient was telling him about her dream

of having been given a golden scarab. Jung, who had his back to the window, in the same moment heard tapping against the glass and, to his surprise, turned to see a scarabaeid beetle (the common rose-chafer), a relative of the scarab, banging on the window. The scarab is an Egyptian symbol of the solar cycle and of rebirth (or transformation), and the patient's exclusively rational perspective on her situation was transformed by the episode.

Another of Jung's examples concerned the pendulum clock that was said to have stopped at the moment when Frederick the Great of Prussia died in 1786. The stopping of clocks at the moment of their owners' death is thought to be a common phenomenon, and may symbolize the ending of time, and the cessation of the heartbeat.

Similarly, there are many accounts of mirrors or pictures falling to the floor and breaking when there is a death, symbolic of the shattering of the earthly image.

COINCIDENCES AT THE SAME TIME IN DIFFERENT PLACES

Leaps of discovery sometimes occur simultaneously in different places; according to the biologist Rupert Sheldrake, this is due to archetypal patterns influencing structural development. The phenomenon was described by Ken Keyes in his book *The Hundredth Monkey* (1981). Japanese scientists had been studying the monkey *Macaca fuscata* for over 30 years, when in 1952 they observed a female monkey develop a new behaviour: she began to wash sweet potatoes in a stream before

BELOW AND BELOW RIGHT Flashes of light and reflections in water are examples of the way movement and light can attract us, and "flirt" for our attention.

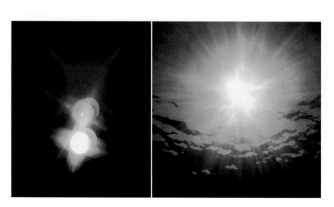

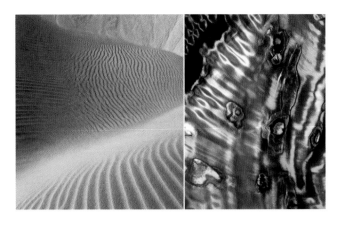

eating them. This new skill was learned by the mothers and young monkeys, though not by the older monkeys, but in 1958 there was a sudden expansion of the activity across the entire population of monkeys on the island. More surprisingly, it seemed that it also jumped simultaneously to monkey colonies on other islands, and to the monkeys on the mainland. Sheldrake has suggested that this phenomenon was connected to a change in the archetypal pattern when a critical mass was reached.

Having spent twenty years formulating his theory of the origin of species, in 1858 Charles Darwin received a letter from the naturalist Alfred Russel Wallace, containing a brief but very similar explanation of the way in which species evolved through natural selection. Wallace was working in the Malay Archipelago, and had come to his conclusions independently of Darwin's work.

COINCIDENCE AT DIFFERENT TIMES
As a persuasive example of the foreknowledge of dreams, Jung relates the dream of a student friend of his, whose father had offered him a trip to Spain if he passed his exams. He became so excited that he dreamed about Spain, seeing himself walking along a street leading to a square where he saw a Gothic cathedral. Upon turning a corner he saw an elegant horse-drawn carriage. When he awoke, he told his friends of the dream, and after passing his exams, he went to Spain, and was greatly surprised

to find the square, the cathedral and the carriage from his dream.

The first Neanderthal fossil bones were discovered in 1856 by quarry workers in the Neander Valley in Germany, and the early humans were named after the valley. By coincidence, the area had been named in the 17th century after a local pastor, Joachim Neumann, who adopted the Greek pseudonym Neander, meaning "new man".

THE FLIRT
Arnold Mindell uses the word "flirt" to describe the interchange and reflection of dreamlike signals between the observer and the observed, whereby it becomes impossible to determine which came first – the sense that an object is asking for attention or the observation itself. Mindell suggests that we have different kinds of attention and awareness. We pay most attention to a consensual reality, but at the edge of this experience many signals flirt for our "second attention". These "flirts" may be a signpost to another reality: a bird swooping, the glint of light on water, or an imagined tear in a friend's eye. Mindell sees flirts as coming from a sentient realm equivalent to Jung's collective unconscious, a pre-signal level where things exist as tendencies before they become manifest. He describes this realm as something like a root system between two trees that are so intertwined it is impossible to separate them.

The belief that the earth and people are deeply connected underpins all shamanic practice,

and is shared by many indigenous peoples. Mindell tells of an Australian Aborigine describing the mysterious power of a tree, which draws our attention, talking to us and telling us a story. A Romany shaman has described his initiation, lying in a field in order to connect to the earth and find his true path, and Native American vision quests are based upon the principle of synchronicities and flirts in nature coming to the inquirer.

The concepts of synchronicity and flirts presuppose that all life is fundamentally connected. This is not yet commonly accepted by mainstream science, and yet developments in quantum physics and field and process-oriented psychological research are pointing in this direction.

ABOVE The playfulness of nature shows itself in these iridescent shell patterns.

ABOVE LEFT Nature is full of rhythms and patterns. Modern science is showing that acausal connections exist through time and space.

BELOW A single falling leaf catching the light as it descends can flirt for our attention.

SYMBOLISM IN SOCIETY

A SYMBOL MAY BE NATURAL OR AN ARTEFACT, AND SYMBOLISM CAN ARISE THROUGH ACTIONS, GESTURES, THOUGHTS OR FEELINGS TO REPRESENT AN UNDERLYING CONCEPT. HOWEVER, THE MEANING OF A SYMBOL IS NOT INTRINSIC IN THE THING ITSELF, BUT RELIES ON ITS CULTURAL AND HISTORICAL CONTEXT AND CAN CHANGE OVER TIME AND SPACE.

MEANING AND CONNECTION

ABOVE Street signs use a "visual shorthand" of pictures, letters and numbers to convey practical information.

TOP For motorists throughout the world, a red traffic light is the universal symbol for "stop".

In the 20th century, theories began to be developed about the meaning and origins of signs and symbols in human society. The American philosopher Charles Sanders Pierce (1839–1914) and the Swiss linguist Ferdinand De Saussure (1857–1913) were the founding fathers of semiotics, the philosophical study of signs and sign systerms, and the way in which meaning is produced and exchanged within a culture.

SEMIOTICS

Pierce referred to three types of signs: "iconic" signs, or those that clearly represent the objects they depict (for instance, a road sign showing the silhouette of a car and a motorcycle); "indexical" signs, which represent concepts that we have learned to associate with a particular sign (for instance, smoke is an index of "fire"); and "symbolic" signs, whose meanings are determined by convention and do not resemble the original object to which they refer (for instance, the international symbol for nuclear waste – three black triangles in a circle on a yellow background – or a red traffic light to indicate "stop"). Pierce noted that as people view the world through the filter of personal and cultural experience, the same symbol can

hold different meanings for different people.

Pierce's contemporary, De Saussure, applied this theory more specifically to language, which is itself a system of signs that endeavours to communicate information and meaning. De Saussure identified two parts of a sign: the "signifier" (the actual sign itself) and the "signified" (the conceptual meaning ascribed to it, which is arrived at by cultural convention). For instance, the letter formation c-a-t (the signifier) in the English language describes a furry animal with four legs, a tail and whiskers, that purrs and miaows (the signified). The signifier is a symbolic sign: the same letter formation could just as easily be used to represent anything else, while to a non-English speaker, it may mean nothing at all.

CULTURAL CONVENTIONS

While this may seem obvious, for De Saussure the implications were profound, extending far beyond the reaches of simple word formations. He argued that the signs we use may appear to be arbitrary, but in fact embody

RIGHT There are many different words for "cat", each suggesting a slightly different meaning.

cultural ideologies and values that we then come to think of as "norms". This view shifted the emphasis away from the notion that there is some kind of objective reality "out there" to the idea that "reality" is always encoded, that the way we perceive and make sense of the world is through the codes of our own culture.

De Saussure also pointed out that meanings operate within a paradigm; we choose signs from a whole range of alternatives. To use the earlier example again, there are several alternative signifiers – puss, pussy, moggy, puss-cat, kitty – that we could use instead of "cat", each one of which confers a slightly different nuance of meaning. Semioticians such as De Saussure have argued that we live among and relate not to physical objects and events, but to systems of signs with

RIGHT Structuralism examines the language of fashion and how our perceptions are formed by sets of signals, this image of a punk rocker could signal either beauty or danger.

meanings. These meanings are not "natural" or inevitable but are embedded in our social structure and value systems.

STRUCTURALISM

De Saussure had examined language as a structure, arguing that this method could equally be applied to any system of making meaning: a set of signals or codes, such as the rules of a game; a tribal or community ritual (a wedding, a rain dance, a funeral); "fashion" (in clothes, food and possessions); and the visual arts, literature, advertising and cinema.

De Saussure's work had far-reaching implications, within not only linguistics, but also the study of all communication. It influenced sociology and was taken up by the leading proponents of the Structuralist movement, the anthropologist Claude Lévi-Strauss (b.1908) and the philosopher Roland Barthes (1915–80).

De Saussure had asserted that a signifying system is any structure or system or organization that creates meaning out of cultural signs. As an anthropologist, Lévi-Strauss applied these ideas to kinship systems, cultural organizations and myth, while Roland Barthes explored contemporary Western cultural "signs", particularly in the realms of food, advertising and clothing.

KINSHIP SYSTEMS

Lévi-Strauss came to the conclusion that regardless of content, all systems of cultural organization share the same fundamental structures. One of these is kinship: every society has had some system for deciding who can marry whom, who can inherit what and from whom, and how these relationships are named. A kinship system is a structure that contains units (men, women and children) who are labelled (fathers, mothers, children), with rules for connecting them; this can be represented visually as a genealogical chart.

Kinship systems structure how goods, people and ideas are "exchanged" within a culture; for example, family groups may "give" women to another family in exchange for something of value (a dowry). Lévi-Strauss insisted that relationships within the structure occur in pairs, which are either similar or opposite. In his book *The Raw and the Cooked* (1964), Lévi-Strauss argues that binary pairs, particularly opposites, form the basic structure of all human cultures (man and woman, for instance) and ways of thought (good and evil). He notes that in every pair, one term is favoured over the other – the "cooked" (culture and civilization) is better than the "raw" (natural and "primitive"), good is preferred to evil, light to dark, and male (in many cultures) to female.

Like Jung, Lévi-Strauss was also interested in explaining why myths from different cultures seemed so similar. Rather than looking at their content, he applied a structural analysis, arguing that structure is what they share. Like language, a myth is made of units that are put together according to certain rules or conventions (such as repetition, the telling of the story in layer after layer), and these units form relationships with each other, based on binary pairs or opposites, which provide the basis of the structure.

ABOVE A wedding, like any other ritual in any other society, has its own set of rules or signals that are similar to the rules or signals of a language.

BELOW Fast food is a hallmark of modern society, while fresh fruit and vegetables symbolize natural goodness and are associated with health.

MYTHOLOGIES

Between 1954 and 1956, Roland Barthes produced a series of 54 articles on a variety of subjects for a French left-wing magazine. Collectively entitled "Mythologies", they provide insights into Barthes' ideas about the construction of meaning, especially in popular culture – films, advertising, newspapers and magazines, photography, cars, children's toys and popular pastimes. Barthes was fascinated by the meaning of things that surround us in everyday life and wanted to challenge their seeming "innocence" and "naturalness". For instance, a sports car and an unpretentious family vehicle share the same functional utility – they are both means of transport – but they connote different things about their owners. It was these secondary signals that Barthes explored, concerned to analyse what he referred to as the "myths" that circulate in contemporary society and that construct the world and our place in it.

ROLES AND RELATIONSHIPS

ABOVE Cigarette smoking by western women in the early 20th century was associated with women's growing independence and equality.

BELOW The symbolism of the veil has varied in different times and places according to social, religious and political conditions.

Social-role theory of the 1960s showed that in any community various roles tend to arise. The successful functioning of the community relies upon the interactions of all these roles, and each one is defined in terms of its relation to all the other roles. Each role is a living symbol of the cultural values of the community.

As societies have become more complex, so too have the role structures within them. In modern societies it is increasingly that an individual will occupy true multiple roles, over time and even simultaneously. A great deal of symbolism is used in defining human roles and role changes, making use of such pointers as uniform, social behaviour or symbolic rites and rituals marking role transition.

Early role theory described roles as social constructs determined by social expectations and the values that needed to be fulfilled within a community. Culturally defined gender roles, particularly, were seen to govern family and occupational activities. More recent theories suggest that roles are also determined by field patterns in nature; they recognize "ghost roles", which, though not explicit, represent undercurrents of feeling in a community.

AGE AND GENDER

In societies where survival is not a given, roles tend to be fewer in number and clearly delineated by gender and age. In more complex societies there is more variation of roles, and more specialization. Complex societies tend to have a greater need of symbols such as uniforms, conventions or rules of conduct to frame the roles.

In the Native American Comanche society, a hunting and warrior people, a boy was expected to be aggressive and to seize what was his. But as he grew older his role changed towards eldership, and he was expected to settle disputes and avoid making enemies unnecessarily. His role became one of wisdom, gentleness and endurance.

In patriarchal societies throughout the world, women and children have held less privileged roles than men, with consequential fights for the rights of both women and children. The 19th-century American reformer Elizabeth Cady Stanton wore Turkish trousers instead of a restricting crinoline; they were taken up by, and named after, Amelia Bloomer, who promoted them as a symbol of the women's rights movement.

The emancipation of women in Iran has been a complex process in which clothing has also been a central symbol. Women came to the fore during the anti-Shah movement, during which their black veils became revolutionary symbols. Upon establishing an Islamic republic, the veil once again became a part of the state's definition of women. Modern Islamist feminists are now trying to differentiate between patriarchal tradition and the values of Islam, with the veil now a complex symbol, often meaning different things to different people, affected by religion, culture or gender.

Many North American tribes honoured the role of the *berdache*, a man or woman whose gender identity differed from his or her sex. Berdaches symbolized spiritual power, were natural "go-betweens" in gender disputes, and were consulted by tribal elders, as they were thought to be connected to the Great Spirit.

RANK AND PRIVILEGE

All societies have systems of rank and associated privileges that are related to the predominant values and beliefs of the culture. Among the Iban of Borneo, for example,

the witch doctor works with the extremes of society, with life and death and the healing of the sick, interacting directly with the spirit world. His role gives him a high rank in the tribe, represented by his elegant feathered headdresses, jewellery and masks.

Sometimes ranking systems are in place for the good of the whole society, and at other times they represent biases within the society, in favour of some people and opposing others. Gypsies have suffered discrimination worldwide, and studies show how they have been subtly ranked as "other" and therefore inferior, by associating them with animals. In India, the Hindu caste system rigidly defines the roles and interactions in traditional society, prohibiting marriage, socialization or even physical contact between members of different castes.

ROLE PLAY AND ROLE MODELS

People need positive role models in order to find the path of their own development. Through role play and role modelling children are able to learn about the roles they are growing into by playing them out in games.

Social learning theory teaches that a major part of child development occurs through role models. The child observes that a role model, often of the same sex, is successful or rewarded in society for their behaviour. The child then adopts the characteristics of the model, and finally identifies more fully with the characteristics of the role, which become his or her own.

BOTTOM RIGHT A common theme in the discrimination against gypsies is that their differences make them inferior to settled societies.

RIGHT Michael Jordan has been an important role model for young black men, particularly in the United States of America.

Public figures often serve as role models, usually for other people of the same sex, gender, race or physical ability. The outstanding basketball player Michael Jordan, for example, serves as a powerful role model to black boys in America. Celebrities may become legends or icons when they come to symbolize or model specific values for other people's lives. The role model symbolizes what a young person (or an adult) might aspire to. But while many role models are famous people, some of the most important role models may be found within our personal circle: they may be parents, older siblings or other family members, teachers or friends.

CHANGING ROLES

Roles and their symbolism change within the bounds of a culture as its values shift. In Western society, it has been traditional for a woman getting married to wear engagement and wedding rings, and adopt her husband's surname to indicate her changed role. In recent decades, however, these customs have ceased to be universal, and new symbols of marriage are emerging. Women no longer automatically change their surname and couples now wear matching rings as symbols of mutual and equal commitment.

Roles may change gradually, mirroring cultural trends, or their overturning may define an abrupt or violent change, such as the deposition of a monarch during a revolution, or the transformation of intellectuals into farm labourers during China's Cultural Revolution in the 1970s.

TABOOS

ABOVE In this 8th-century banner of the Buddha preaching, he is insulated from touching the ground, as if his spiritual energy would be drained away by contact with the earth.

BELOW Lot's daughters, believing that all other men had been destroyed, felt forced to disregard the taboo of incest and trick their father into having sex with them by getting him drunk.

The word "taboo" comes from the Polynesian *tabu*, which is a system of prohibiting actions or the use of objects because they are considered either sacred or dangerous, unclean or accursed. Taboos may emerge from a moral consciousness and motivate individual and collective moral conscience, but they may also be used to maintain social hierarchies and order.

In animist and nature-based societies, the origin of taboos probably relates to the likes and dislikes of the various levels of spirits in relation to one another. In later cultures, taboos relate more to the people's attempts to appease their gods and goddesses. Within contemporary society, the word taboo has less spiritual significance, and more generally refers to things that are not allowed or not done within society for various social reasons.

PROTECTING DIVINITY

In many cultures, royalty has been seen as divine, and royal individuals have been protected from mundane reality by never being required to touch the

ground. They would be carried on the backs or shoulders of others, on an animal or in a carriage, or would walk on carpets specially laid for them.

Montezuma, the Aztec emperor of Mexico, was always carried by his noblemen and never once set foot on the ground. Early kings and queens of Uganda never set foot outside the beautiful enclosures within which they lived. The king of Persia walked on carpets upon which only he could tread. Even today there is a worldwide custom of rolling out a red carpet for royalty on ceremonial occasions.

INCEST TABOOS

Incest – having sexual relations with someone who is a close relation – is a form of taboo that is found worldwide, probably because of the genetic defects it often leads to. Native American and Chinese cultures extend the idea of incest to having relations with people with the same family name. However, gods and royalty are often exempt in order to keep the royal or divine blood pure. While Freud interpreted incest

literally, and sexuality as a potentially dangerous force requiring taboo to avoid its dangers, Jung viewed incest as a symbolic image referring to the attempt of the individual to return to the mother's womb to be reborn.

Incest is a common mythological theme among gods, goddesses and royalty, and particularly in societies that are focused on maintaining their supremacy. When rulers are seen as divine, marrying someone outside the family would sully the pure royal blood. The Egyptian goddess Isis married her brother Osiris. Queen Cleopatra herself was the result of seven generations of brother–sister marriages. In the Old Testament Lot's daughters have sex with their father because there is no other male available to impregnate them. Inca rulers were allowed to marry their sisters.

GENDER TABOOS

In the traditional Kung Bushman society of the Kalahari, where living conditions are very harsh, social roles are strongly divided according to gender. The men hunt, and make weapons and fire, and the woman build a shelter for the family, prepare food, keep the fire and keep the house in order. The separation of their roles is emphasized by assigning different sides of the fire for where men and women should sit. If a woman sits in a man's place, it is thought she will succumb to a mysterious illness, and if the man sits on the woman's side of the fire, his hunting powers might be

lessened. It is also thought that if women touch a man's weapons, his power will lessen.

TABOO FOOD AND ANIMALS

In many cultures it has been believed that spirits could enter or possess inanimate objects, which then become objects of worship, or fetishes. When edible fruits or plants became fetishes they became taboo as food. As an example, the Levantine peoples never ate apples because they believed them to be inhabited by a nature spirit. Animals that were capable of eating human flesh would become a fetish; thus the dog became a taboo animal for the Parsees. Eating apes and monkeys is taboo in many societies because their appearance is similar to that of humans. Both the Phoenicians and the Jews considered the serpent a channel for evil spirits.

In ancient Egypt, animals were worshipped and cared for as vessels of good or evil powers. Their gods were considered incarnate in particular species, which were then protected by taboo. Like Jews and Moslems, they considered the pig an unclean animal, possibly because of its habit of scavenging. It was thought that if a pig was touched in passing, the person should immediately plunge themself in water for purification. Egyptian swineherds were considered of low caste and were not allowed to enter temples.

The cow is considered sacred in Hindu India, where it is a living symbol of motherhood due to its ability to produce milk. The feeding of the cow is therefore an act of worship. The majority of Hindus are vegetarian, and it is particularly taboo to kill or eat cows. As a result they may commonly be seen wandering the streets undisturbed. Even the urine from a cow is seen as sacred, and is sometimes used in purification rituals for people who have transgressed a taboo.

In societies where animals take on the role of totems, there are taboos against people eating or killing animals to whose totem clans they belong. In identifying with the animal, a person becomes a relative or guardian of the animal. However, another member of the community with a different animal familiar may freely hunt and eat the animal. The Euahlayi people of New South Wales and southern Queensland believe that a child who eats their own animal familiar by accident will become sick: in the case of taboo plains bustard or turkey eggs, this could result in the loss of sight, while eating taboo kangaroo flesh could cause their skin to break out in sores and their limbs to wither. However, while it is taboo for the Euahlayi to eat their animal familiar, it is acceptable to eat the totem animal of their clan.

MENSTRUATION TABOOS

Within patriarchal societies, menstruation has commonly been taboo, both in the ancient and the modern world. However, in matriarchal societies, which revered the female body, menstruation was considered a powerful and healing process. It has also been associated with great feminine powers. The menstrual cycle and the cycles of the moon were measured in pre-patriarchal times on wooden sticks that historians have called "calendar sticks". One possible origin of the menstruation taboo may be the fear that women could control the tides and seasonal changes through the monthly cycles of their bodies.

The Jews of the ancient world believed that menstrual blood had poisonous qualities. The Old Testament includes a prohibition against contact with it: Leviticus records that Moses received word from God that a man who sleeps with a menstruating woman should be cut off from his people, and that menstruating women are unclean for seven days.

Freud related the menstrual taboo to a negative view of women, whereas Bruno Bettelheim suggested that both the ability to bear children and to menstruate evoked intense envy in men, who created taboos in an attempt to make the sexes more equal. Feminists have called this "womb envy", partly as a protest against Freud's theory that women suffer "penis envy".

POST-PARTUM BLOOD

In many parts of the world the blood that accompanies childbirth has been seen as unclean, perhaps because a woman giving birth, and the new baby, were believed to be in close contact with spirits and other worlds. Some cultures have cleansing rituals for removing the blood.

ABOVE For Hindus it is taboo to kill or eat a cow.

TOP The apple, a Judaeo-Christian forbidden fruit.

GROUP IDENTITY

ABOVE Every detail of a flag is symbolic – its colour, pattern and design, and motifs.

FLEUR-DE-LYS

Most commonly associated with French royalty and the right to rule France, the fleur-de-lys (lily flower) has three petals, standing for both the Holy Trinity and the triple majesty of God, creation and royalty.

Symbolism has always been used to denote identity and to confirm adherence to social groups or "families", the basic units of society. Whether based on shared beliefs or common interests and activities, all organized groups – whether at a local, regional, national or international level – have their own symbols of identity. These may be in the shapes of totems, banners, flags or standards, or expressed through dress codes or through the observance of certain ritualized forms of behaviour. One of the important features of such symbolism is its visibility: it is designed to provide an instantly recognizable sign of group identity, a way of codifying and structuring social relations, of creating a distinction between who's "in" and who's "out", and to stir an emotional response, such as fear, respect, humility or pride, in all who see it.

LEADERSHIP

When people started to form large groups to live and hunt together, a leader was appointed to rule them and settle disputes.

As a mark of office, a leader might wear a ceremonial headdress and hold a long decorated staff, rod or spear, topped with an emblem. The staff was also used as a visible sign to rally around or to point out the direction of a march or attack. These early "flags" are known as vexilloids, and originally were made of wood, feathers and other animal pieces (bones, horns, skins). Aztec vexilloids, for instance, made extensive use of green quetzal feathers, and were decorated with precious metals such as gold, silver and copper, and precious stones. Today tribes in New Guinea use vexilloids that consist mostly of wood and dried grass, with emblems of painted wood, feathers and bits of cloth.

FLAGS

In China the invention of silk fabric led to the creation of banners, which were easier to carry and more visible from a distance than vexilloids. From China, the use of fabric flags spread to Europe, where they were first used as military and ceremonial signs, but later as a

way of identifying rulers, their domains and nationality at sea. The 17th century saw the introduction of standardized regimental colours, war ensigns, jacks (the square flags hoisted up the "jackstaff" on a ship) and the house flags of the trading companies (a precursor of the modern logo). The first national flags on land appeared in the last quarter of the 18th century. During the 19th and 20th centuries, a host of other flags also appeared: of government agencies and officials; provincial flags; rank flags in all branches of the armed forces; and flags of schools, universities, scientific institutions, organizations, political parties, trades unions and guerrilla movements. There are also flags of ethnic groups, business corporations and sporting clubs.

All the elements of a flag are symbolic – its colours, motifs and overall design – and there are many customs surrounding flag etiquette. For instance, in a military parade, flags are saluted when being hoisted, lowered or passed; flying a flag at half-mast is a sign of mourning; a pall flag laid over a coffin, used mainly at government and military funerals, is a symbol of national respect for the deceased; desecrating a flag is a punishable offence in most countries of the world.

TRIBE AND NATION

In traditional societies, clans and tribes have used a variety of symbolic devices to distinguish one group from another. For instance, among many Native

OCCUPATIONS AND PROFESSIONS

For many people, membership of a trade or profession is a symbol of identity, conferring rank and social status through belonging to that particular group. Many traditional occupations can be recognized by generic symbols – for instance a chef's hat, a barber's pole, a pawnbroker's three golden balls, a sailor's anchor – while almost every modern commercial enterprise has its own distinctive company logo. Many professions are also instantly recognizable by their dress codes – the formal uniforms of the armed forces, the blue overalls of a manual worker, the dark suit and tie of a city worker or the white coat of a laboratory technician – while special titles may be used to denote hierarchy within the group, such as doctor, professor, lieutenant, sergeant or chief executive officer (CEO).

Americans totems (natural objects, such as animals) are used to represent particular lodges and tribes, as well as individuals, while each clan of the Scottish Highlanders has its own tartan (a type of checked fabric) design. In medieval heraldry, most European rulers adopted coats of arms and armorial banners bearing one of the two most important heraldic figures: the lion (king of beasts) or the eagle (king of Heaven). The fleur-de-lys, another frequent heraldic motif, was particularly associated with the French court; it was later adopted by the international Boy Scout movement. Today many nations continue to be associated with a particular emblem: for instance, the USA with the bald-headed eagle, Canada with the maple leaf and England with the Tudor Rose.

There are also many nations without statehood (for instance in the USA there are more than 550 federally recognized nations and tribes) who have their own emblem of identity. For instance, eleven Sioux tribes living in South Dakota share a common white flag. The flag's central compass emblem symbolizes the Native American Medicine Wheel (and the four directions, the four seasons and the four elements) and is surrounded by eleven tepees, representing the number of tribes. There are also many groups within mainstream society who have chosen a symbol to identify themselves. For instance, in the West, the colour pink has been adopted by gay people, black by some racial and political groups, and green by the environmental movement.

POLITICS AND REBELLION

Political groups, rebellions and revolutions have always been associated with particular symbols. At the end of the 15th century, German peasants rebelled under a white pennant with the emblem of a golden peasant shoe, the Bundschuh, which in contrast to the boots worn by the nobility was a symbol of peasantry. Communism and fascism, two of the most influential political movements of the 20th century, also both made use of symbols. The symbol of communism was the hammer and sickle, representing the alliance between

THE SWASTIKA

Hitler adopted the swastika, an ancient solar symbol with many profound meanings, as the sign for the Nazi party. The distinctive black sign in a white circle against a red background became the German national flag in 1935, and the emblem was used in many different places – including on children's toys – to promote Nazi propaganda and instil allegiance to Hitler. Today, some neo-Nazi groups continue to use the swastika or a three-legged variation as an emblem of identity.

industrial and agricultural workers; for most of the 20th century, the hammer and sickle was the emblem of the Russian flag and the world's first communist state.

Fascism is a nationalist movement led by a dictator. It is named after the "fasces" symbol that was worn as a badge by the Italian dictator Benito Mussolini (1883–1945). The fasces comprised a bundle of birch or elm rods, bound by a red cord, sometimes wrapped around an axe, a symbol of justice, scourging and decapitation. It dates back to ancient Rome, when it was carried by lictors, officials who had the power to pronounce sentence. Hitler, however, used a different symbol for his fascist Nazi party: the swastika.

ABOVE The hammer and sickle is a communist symbol, standing for the union of industrial and agricultural workers.

TOP The word fascism is derived from "fasces", the bundle of rods carried by Roman officials.

TRADITIONAL STORYTELLING

THE ART OF LISTENING

In some South American storytelling traditions, it is said that humans are possessed of a gift of hearing that goes beyond the ordinary. This is the soul's way of paying attention and learning. The story-makers, or cantadoras, of old spun mythical tales of mystery in order to wake up the sleeping soul, wanting it to prick up its ears and tune in to the wisdom contained within the story's telling.

ABOVE The mermaid embodies a deep connection between woman and the sea.

BELOW Noah's Ark, a symbol of man's faith and hope when faced with life-destroying disaster.

From the earliest times, human beings have used stories to describe things they could not explain otherwise. Such stories attempt to answer some of the most fundamental questions about human existence – about why we are here and where we are going, about the nature of the world around us and how we fit into it.

Every culture has formulated its own poetic visions and sacred narratives – the metaphorical understandings that we refer to as myths. The word "myth" is derived from the Greek *mythos*, meaning word or story, but it has come to stand for a narrative that helps to explain the origin and character of a culture in symbolic terms. The meaning and content of such stories will vary across time and place, and from person to person, but one of the functions of myth is to celebrate the ambiguities and contradictions at the heart of human existence.

THE STORYTELLER

Long before myths were written down, they were transmitted by word of mouth. In order to survive the passage of time, they had to be presented as good, memorable stories, appealing to one generation after another, possibly evolving to adapt to new social needs. Storytelling could take place almost anywhere – in the home, in the marketplace or at the royal court – and traditionally the art of storytelling was highly valued, since it was the means by which a culture's social codes and values, its

ancestral lineage and history, and its connection to the divine were kept alive. The storyteller played a vital role in the community, sometimes as an official of a royal or noble court, sometimes as a wandering minstrel who travelled from place to place, delivering stories that were entertaining and instructive. Many religious figures, including Jesus and Mohammed, used storytelling as a vehicle for their teachings.

STORYTELLING RITUALS

The style or protocol of storytelling varies from culture to culture. In many traditional African societies, the audience feels free to interrupt, make criticisms or suggest improved versions to the storyteller. Throughout Africa, a common storytelling form is the "call and response", whereby a "caller" raises a "song" and the chorus in the community participate and respond to the call.

When the San people of the Kalahari tell stories about particular animals, they mimic the formation of the animals' mouths, pronouncing their words as the animals might, as a way of keeping in touch with and honouring the spirit of the animal. Smoking a pipe and passing it from person to person is often a part of storytelling rituals among Native American peoples, such as the Algonquin. According to the Algonquin, "if we cease sharing our stories, our knowledge becomes lost". In many parts of the world today, people are rediscovering the

THE VALKYRIE

In Norse myth, the Valkyries were supernatural women, death angels who hovered over the battlefields granting victory or defeat to warriors. After death, they took the spirits of the valiant slain to Odin's realm of Valhalla.

THE UNDERWORLD

Very often the underworld lies across a stretch of water, such as the River Styx of Greek mythology. The dead are often ferried across on a boat (such as the funeral barques of Egyptian wall paintings, or the ship of the Viking warrior, launched at death out to sea), when they will be judged for their actions in their earthly life. A common symbol for judgement is the weighing of the soul: the ancient Egyptians believed the dead person's heart was weighed before Osiris, lord of the underworld.

power of storytelling to make sense of their lives and to keep the connection with their cultural and ancestral lineage alive.

MYTHIC THEMES

Questions about life and death are explored through myth, and stories of the origins and the end of the world can be found in all cultures. Creation myths refer to a primal chaos, symbolized in many cultures as a watery, dark and mysterious place. Myths also anticipate the destruction of the world in a catastrophic event – such as the Norse cataclysm Ragnarok – while many refer to an earlier time when the world was nearly destroyed by a deluge. The Biblical story of Noah is the best-known example; in a similar Mesopotamian tale, Utnapishtim, a wise man who alone survived the flood, was made an immortal.

Typically, myths are tales of divine and semi-divine beings – gods and goddesses, heroes and heroines – archetypal figures who act out the struggle between good and evil, exploring moral conflicts and powerful human emotions such as desire and greed, jealousy and lust, ambition, love and hate. Notions of an underworld and an afterlife, as well as a magical otherworldly realm, are common, and animals with extraordinary powers helping humankind feature in many myths.

ANIMALS IN MYTH

Mythologies from around the world feature animals in one form or another, and they have often been deified. In ancient Egypt, shrines were set up for the worship of sacred beasts such as the Ram of Mendes and the Bull of Apis, while at one time, cobras and vultures were the prime deities of Lower and Upper Egypt respectively. In Africa, particular tribes and chiefs trace their ancestry back to an animal god. For instance, Haile Selassie (the "Lion of Judah"), founding father of the Rastafarian religion and one-time emperor of Ethiopia, traced his lineage back to the powerful god Simba the lion, while some Zulu chiefs claim descent from the python.

Creatures that are half-human and half-animal also appear in many cultures, such as Garuda, the eagle with the body of a man in Hindu mythology, or the centaurs and mermaids of classical myth. The hybrid man-horse centaur has been used to symbolize man trapped by his own sensual impulses, especially lust and violence.

In the stories of many other cultures, animals and humans enjoy a more symbiotic relationship: in Native American myths, animals are often addressed as "brother", while in the Arctic regions, there is a

spiritual relationship between humans and the animals that are vital for the community's survival.

Animals sometimes appear as trickster figures in traditional stories; Coyote is the trickster god of the Native Americans and can change his form at will, while African stories feature Hare (Brer Rabbit in America) and Anansi, the spider. Such characters break the rules of nature, or the gods, though usually with positive results, and perhaps represent the irrepressibility and inventiveness of the human spirit.

MODELS OF SOCIETY

Mythology often reinforces and justifies relations of power and leadership. Typically this is explored through a pantheon with a hierarchical structure: a supreme god and/or goddess at the head (often associated with the heavens and the earth) followed by a host of greater and lesser deities. This structure follows that adopted by the human society. In China, for instance, Heaven was visualized as a bureaucracy, maintaining law and order in the same way as the imperial administration. In Japan, the tale of Izanagi and Izanami

ABOVE Odysseus's epic journey symbolizes individual endeavour, but also stands as a metaphor for the cycle of life.

ABOVE Centaurs are used to symbolize lust: the trap of animal sexual impulse.

ABOVE The cobra has a protective aspect in myth and sacred tradition.

ABOVE In some Native American traditions, the coyote is associated with evil, winter and death.

LEFT In Greek myth, a siren is a demonic figure, part woman part fish, which uses its song to enchant sailors and lure them to their death.

CELTIC BARD

Responsibility for passing on Celtic tribal history, legend and folklore lay with the bard. The earliest bards on record include Aneirin and Taliesin from the 6th century AD. Stories were presented in the form of poems and songs as well as narratives, and the bard's skill was highly valued, in particular a quality called *hwyl* in Welsh – the passion that could inspire an audience. Today the Celtic bardic tradition is continued at Welsh cultural festivals called *eisteddfodau*.

(the first man and woman) served to justify women's alleged inferiority to men, although there are hints that originally Japan may have been organized on a matriarchal lineage, with the imperial family claiming descent from the sun goddess Amaterasu right up until the end of World War II in 1945.

The relationship of deities to one another is explained in human terms of kinship, love and hatred, competition and influence, with each deity responsible for a particular area of human life – fertility, childbirth, love and relationship, war and conflict, the arts, wealth and prosperity. Many stories of Greco-Roman myth concern the interactions of the gods – with humans often used as pawns in their power games (explaining the apparent randomness of good and

bad luck) – while rivalry between the gods is evident in Norse myth. In all these stories the gods exhibit character traits and behaviour that are entirely representative of human nature.

Veneration of the ancestors is an important part of the structure of many traditional societies, and thus features prominently in their mythologies; in Australian Aboriginal mythology, for example, it is the ancestors of the Dreamtime who are said to have shaped the landscape and determined the entire nature of the animal and human world.

HEROIC FIGURES

The exploits and journeys of heroic figures are frequently the subject of myth. Many owe their superhuman powers to some divine connection: Kintaro, the warrior hero of Japanese myth, was the son of a mountain spirit; Rama, in the Hindu epic the Ramayana, was an incarnation of the god Vishnu, while Heracles,

perhaps the greatest of the Greek heroes, was the son of Zeus. Through their actions and their personal qualities – such as bravery, persistence, patience and unconditional love – the heroes and heroines of myth offer a pattern on which people can model themselves.

Some myths show how humans can aspire to the divine: in China, Taoist myths of the Eight Immortals describe how, through their piety and devotion, the Immortals manage to earn everlasting life in Heaven; while Heracles, through his famous twelve labours (tasks given him as punishment for an early crime), became the only Greek hero to achieve immortality.

The medieval Celtic myth of King Arthur and his Knights of the Round Table was centred on the quest for the Holy Grail, said

BELOW The exploits of the divine hero, Rama and his wife Sita (an incarnation of Lakshmi) are told in the Ramayana.

RIGHT As punishment for giving the
divine energy of fire to humans,
Zeus bound Prometheus to a rock
for eternity.

to be the chalice used by Christ at
the Last Supper, or used to catch
his blood at the Crucifixion
(though it also had pre-Christian
roots, in the Celtic theme of the
magic cauldron). The Grail
became a symbol of immortality
and perfection, attainable only
through great virtue.

Many heroic figures are also
"culture heroes", the discoverers
of secrets of nature or of the ideas
and inventions on which a
civilization depends. Examples
include the Greek Prometheus,
who stole fire from the gods and
gave it to humans, and the
Polynesian Maui, who "fished up"
land from the ocean and stole fire
from the underworld.

DANGEROUS WOMEN

Women in myth are often bad,
dangerous or demonic, either
because of their curiosity and
disobedience or because of their
beauty or magic powers. In Greek
myth, Pandora disobeys the gods
and opens a box that unleashes
sickness and evil into the world,
just as in the Judaeo-Christian
tradition, Eve disobeys God and
is held responsible for humans'
expulsion from paradise. The
Sirens of Greek myth, sea
monsters with an insatiable
appetite for blood, lured sailors to
their death by shape-changing
into beautiful maidens, while in
China, demon spirits associated
with violent death were also apt
to disguise themselves as beautiful
girls. In India, it was said that the
true character of a rakshasi
(female demon) could be
recognized by the way her feet
pointed backwards.

MODERN MYTH-MAKING

The myths of the ancient
storytellers continue to resonate
in modern times because they
symbolize aspects of human
nature and interaction that remain
relevant to us, and they are
constantly being reworked and
adapted in art, literature and
popular culture.

Although the tradition of
storytelling as a formal way of
preserving group culture and
myth has largely died out in the
West, many people still use
photograph albums and
scrapbooks to record important
life events through pictures and
words. Psychologists now
recognize this as therapeutic for
people who have lost direct access
to their past through their
families, such as adopted children
or survivors of traumatic events.

THE HERO GILGAMESH

The epic of Gilgamesh is one of the earliest known hero myths and contains many archetypal motifs.
Gilgamesh, King of Uruk in Mesopotamia, was part-human, part-god. He was becoming so arrogant that
the gods created the warrior Enkidu to challenge him. After fighting, the two men became close friends
and together defeated the monster Humbaba. Impressed by his courage and manly beauty, the goddess
Inanna desired Gilgamesh as her lover. When he spurned her, she exacted her revenge by
sending the Bull of Heaven to terrorize Uruk, but together Enkidu and Gilgamesh
struck it dead. The gods demanded that one of the heroes must pay with his life
for the slaughter of the bull, and Enkidu died. Distraught, Gilgamesh set
out on a journey to try to learn why men must die. He travelled to the
underworld and was carried over the bitter waters of death by
Urshanabi, ferryman of the gods. In the underworld he met
Utnapishtim, the immortal ancestor of humankind and the only
man to have survived the great flood, who told him that like
sleep, death comes to us all and is not to be feared. On his
way home, Gilgamesh found a plant that could restore youth,
but as he stopped to drink at a pool, a snake ate the plant.
This is why snakes shed their skins and become young again,
while men age and die. Gilgamesh returned home sadly to tell
his story to his people, forced to resign himself to acceptance
of his fate. His story encapsulates the timeless themes of
human ambition, attachment and loss, the restless questioning
of existence and its purpose, and the inevitability of death.

ART

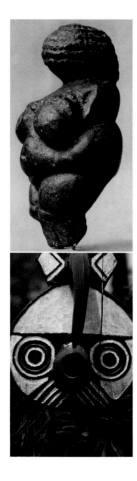

ABOVE Masks are a feature of tribal art, linked with ritual practices and carrying many layers of symbolic meaning.

TOP The Venus of Willendorf, prehistoric Mother goddess.

RIGHT Chinese art contains many symbolic items, much of it linking landscape to the human body or offering spiritual or moral messages.

Since the earliest times, many of humanity's most profound and enduring symbols have been recorded through art. Whether the cave paintings, sculptures and artefacts of tribal art, the highly elaborate creations of the European Renaissance, or movements such as Surrealism, symbols in art have been used in a variety of different ways to express the beliefs and preoccupations of the day. For whether consciously executed or not, it has always been the role of the artist to act as instrument and spokesperson for the spirit of their age, giving form to the nature and values of the time.

TRIBAL ART

The carvings, paintings and compositions of the indigenous peoples of Africa, America, Australia and Oceania have little in common except that they all evolved – like nearly all major artistic forms – in intimate association with religion and magic. Seldom decorative in intention, they are expressions of humanity's common endeavour to live in harmony with, or to control, natural and supernatural forces. Take for instance Easter Island's monolithic heads and half-length figures, sculptures up to 18m (60ft) high that were carved over a long time period (AD 900–1500). These are thought to symbolize the power that throughout Polynesia, ruling chiefs were believed to inherit from the gods and retain after death, when they themselves were deified. Carved and painted wooden masks are a feature of

both African and North American cultures. Some have life-like human faces, others incorporate animal forms, many are mainly animal. Often these are linked with shamanic practices, designed to transform the wearer and connect them to the magic power of the spirit-world, and are used in ritual and ceremony.

Australian Aboriginal art has remained visible at sacred sites over the millennia and has a continuity of tradition, using the surface of the earth, rocks, caves and tree bark as well as the human body to express a world view in which there is no distinction between the secular and the sacred, the natural and the supernatural, past and present, or even the visible and the invisible.

RELIGIOUS SYMBOLISM

The intimate relationship between religion and symbolism is expressed in the art and artefacts of all civilizations. In prehistory, the iconic Venus of Willendorf, a limestone statuette of a

full-breasted nude (c. 24,000–22,000 BC), is believed to be at once a fertility symbol and an archetype of the Great Mother. Other figurines from this period, having similarly exaggerated sexual characteristics, have led to speculation that these early European hunter societies had a matriarchal sacred tradition, venerating the Mother archetype of the Great Goddess.

Thousands of years later in ancient Egypt, funerary art reveals preoccupations with the afterlife, while in medieval Europe, narrative paintings with a multi-layered symbolism were used to instruct the illiterate masses in the Christian Scriptures and to spell out people's relationship with God and the cosmos. Islamic art is non-figurative – representation of living creatures is forbidden, since this would mean representing an aspect of Allah, which is beyond human capability. The art is therefore characterized by repeating geometric patterns and designs. Its only specifically religious

RIGHT The works of Max Ernst, like those of his fellow surrealists, is full of Freudian sexual symbolism.

elements are its Qur'anic inscriptions, a reminder to the faithful that Allah is ever present and supersedes anything created by humans. Conversely, in both Buddhism and Hinduism, an emphasis is placed upon the visual power of symbols to elevate consciousness, and figurative symbolism appears in both traditions. Though the Buddha said he did not want to be worshipped, and early Buddhist art confined itself to representations of his footprint (to symbolize his presence) and of the wheel as a symbol of his teachings, people's desire for an image of the Buddha himself soon took over. One of the most impressive examples (dating from the 5th century AD) is a colossal carving, nearly 14m (45ft) high, cut into the cliff-face at the Longmen cave at Yungang, China, the site of a rock-cut temple.

CHINESE TRADITIONS

Highly stylized forms of symbolic expression are characteristic of Chinese art, which has always sought to inspire and educate the viewer, providing insights into the relationship between humans and the divine. Spiritual and moral messages were conveyed through certain set themes, particularly landscapes and the natural world. For instance, every part of the landscape was believed to symbolize an aspect of being human: water was blood, trees and grass were hair, clouds and mists were clothing, and a solitary wandering scholar was the soul. Bamboo, which can be bent without breaking, represented the

spirit of the scholar, while jade stood for purity. Japanese art also draws on nature for its symbolism: cherry blossom is a frequent motif, a herald of spring and token of good luck, and because of its transience a symbol of mortality.

THE RENAISSANCE

Beginning in 14th-century Italy, the Renaissance (French: "rebirth") represented a renewed interest in the art, architecture and literature of ancient Greece and Rome. Many artists looked to nature, the human body and Greco-Roman mythology for inspiration. For instance, the painting *Primavera* ("Spring") by Sandro Botticelli (1445–1510) recounts the story of the nymph Chloris, pursued by Zephyr, god of the wind, who transforms her into Flora, goddess of spring. At the centre of the painting is the goddess Venus, symbol of the season's fertility, while spring itself is also a metaphor for the Renaissance period, the return of an appreciation for the arts, science and learning.

Biblical themes were also invested with classical symbolism; for instance, in his painting *The Last Judgement*, Michelangelo (1475–1564) glorifies Christ as resplendent Apollo, the Greek sun-god, rather than portraying him as a crucified and suffering saviour. Raphael (1483–1520), who was commissioned to decorate the Vatican, combines the more traditional symbolism of God as a grey-bearded patriarch with mythical satyrs and nymphs in his Loggia.

SURREALISM

Beginning as a literary movement, Surrealism was strongly influenced by Freud's ideas about sexuality, free association, dreams and the subconscious. Sexual symbolism – phallic noses, pubic hair in unexpected places – pervades Surrealist imagery, as painters such as Max Ernst (1891 –1976), René Magritte (1898– 1967) and Salvador Dali (1904–89) tried to represent and liberate the workings of the irrational, subconscious mind, challenging the conventions of artistic Realism and polite society. Magritte intentionally mislabelled his paintings, Ernst created strange landscapes inhabited by extraordinary animals and organic forms, while Dali built up a new language of symbolic imagery of melting watches, spindle-legged creatures, flowers hatching out of eggs and other bizarre images.

ADVERTISING

ABOVE Steve McQueen in *Bullitt* with his 1968 Ford Mustang. Both the man and the car became icons representing rebellious male power.

BELOW Sexual imagery has long been used to sell products. Images of women as sex symbols may be targeted at both men and women, as epitomized in this advertisement for a bra.

Using the powers of persuasion to promote a product is an ancient practice. The symbolism used to persuade or influence people must appeal to the central concerns and beliefs of the consumer. In the modern advertising industry, successful advertisers relate to what people consciously or unconsciously respond to or want to be associated with, and design and package products to ride trends in cultural and personal taste.

While the intrinsic quality of the product and the good reputation of its manufacturer were central factors in early marketing, large-scale mass-production and international trade have distanced the consumer from the product and the producer, and advertising has stepped in to fill the gap, becoming a role and an industry in its own right. Most modern advertising is aimed at promoting an entire brand rather than an individual product, creating a sense of allegiance in its customers by matching its image to them through symbolism.

PSYCHOLOGY IN ADVERTISING

Freudian psychology influenced 20th-century advertising with its ideas about unconscious desires. Advertisers began to use "subliminal persuasion" and "symbolic association" to such a degree that the image or brand name became more important than the product. The car is no longer merely a form of transport: while it is designed to be streamlined and functional, it is also enhanced with feminine curves or phallic frontage to appeal to its potential male buyers. It is advertised as a symbol of status and lifestyle.

In the 1920s Freud's nephew, Edward Bernays, used his uncle's ideas for the manipulation of American public opinion, and is often called "the father of public relations". He showed corporations how they could match people's unconscious desires to their products and turned consumer items into lifestyle symbols: for instance, in a famous stunt of 1929 for the American Tobacco Company, he hired models to parade through the streets of New York, smoking, under the banner of "the torch of freedom". By linking smoking with the drive towards women's liberation, he effectively broke the taboo against American women smoking in public.

SEX IN ADVERTISING

The saying that "sex sells" is equally true of any other imagery that appeals to human emotions, such as the use of people's instinctive response to babies to sell a product. But sexuality is probably the most commonly used "attractor", and is widely used in marketing, both subtly and blatantly. Most advertising uses conventional sex symbols, depicting women as objects of lust and men as dominant.

Both the film and advertising industries continually explore and push the limits of sexual explicitness. Sexual imagery generates the greatest impact, inducing excitement and outrage, when it tugs on the morals and taboos of a given culture.

ADVERTISING AND CINEMATIC INTERFACE

The worlds of advertising and film use symbolism to evoke powerful emotions appealing to the popular culture of the time. These two industries borrow strongly from one another in their use of symbolism and genre: films are used to sell fashion items through product placement, and movie icons are used in advertisements, so that sometimes there seems little difference between the two.

A good example of the interplay of film and advertising is the 1968 film *Bullitt*, which some say starred both Steve McQueen and the 1968 Ford Mustang, both symbols of urban rebellion, toughness and male power. In the 2000s the original footage was cleverly remixed for an advertisement for Ford, creating the illusion of McQueen driving the latest model of the Ford Puma. Thirty years on, the actor's iconic image still had the power to sell a car.

THE CAR – A SYMBOL OF THE INDUSTRIAL AGE

Himself an icon of the industrial age, Henry Ford used mass-production methods to make cars that would not be restricted to a wealthy elite. General Motors overtook the success of Ford when their cars became symbols of the "Roaring Twenties", and were designed and sold as representing the new-found liberation, sexual freedom and self-expression of the "Jazz Age".

During the 1930s depression in the United States, closed cars or sedans conveyed a sober and puritanical image. But this period was soon followed by an explosion of car sales and competition, with the post-war car being sold as a symbol of the "American dream". Advertising now portrayed cars as dream-mobiles, inviting potential owners to fulfil their desires for sex, speed, power, wealth and status.

To this day, cars occupy what Arnold Mindell might call the timespirit of progressiveness and success. Modern car designs and advertising are beginning to play with less gender-stereotyped symbolism, in which androgyny, and the blurring of sexual roles, are explored. Where previously advertising for cars was directed only at men, it is now aimed at both men and women.

CORPORATE IMAGE

A company or business image is considered of great importance in modern marketing. Corporate identity is often expressed symbolically through logos and corporate style, relating to the

"raison d'être" of the organization and to the impression it wishes to give to the outside world. Many apparently modern logos in fact have their roots in ancient symbolism. Tripartite symbols, for instance, which represent harmony and perfection, are used by companies such as Mitsubishi and Mercedes-Benz. The ancient solar cross (an equal-armed cross within a circle) appears on the badges of Fiat and BMW. The golden arches of McDonald's can be interpreted as a giant M, but also match the ancient alchemical sign for fire.

Branding aims to identify the product with producers who can be trusted. Studies of corporate personality have shown the effectiveness of bright bands of colour when used as a part of the brand's image. One such colourful logo is that of Esso/Exxon, which also uses a tiger as a kind of company mascot – its famous slogan, "Put a Tiger In Your Tank", invited the consumer to identify with the power and beauty of the animal.

Company and brand names have significant impact on consumers faced with a market saturated with competing products. Each year the Chairman of the Board of Sony reinforces to staff the idea that the four letters S, O, N and Y are the company's most valuable asset, and that their actions must increase their value.

INTERNATIONAL ADVERTISING

The expansion of global markets has led to new challenges for international advertising, most of which relate to the meaning and values being communicated. One problem is the predominance of Western values and ideals depicted in adverts, which can both influence and offend other cultures. Countries with different moral or religious views often find the images of Western advertising sexually explicit, or disapprove of the roles played by women, and so the advertising may be experienced as subversive.

RIGHT The logo of McDonald's is an adaptation of the alchemical sign for fire, shown beneath.

BELOW In the 1920s car manufacturers presented their products as symbols of wealth, liberation and self-expression.

ABOVE Fiat's logo makes use of the ancient symbol of the sun cross.

TOP The tripartite Mitsubishi logo.

SYMBOLISM AND SCIENCE

THE CLOCK

Since it is closely related to modern concepts of control, productivity and autonomy, the clock is an important functional symbol of the machine age. In the 17th and 18th centuries clocks became sufficiently accurate to measure minutes and seconds, and during this period people shifted away from being guided by the symbolism and rhythms of nature, instead becoming ruled by the clock. The Jungian therapist Marie-Louise von Franz (1915–89) described the clock in post-Cartesian times as coming to symbolize a soulless universe.

BELOW The Copernican view of the universe.

Signs, symbols and symbolism play an important part in scientific research and the development of scientific theories. Scientific concepts are rooted in contemporary or emerging beliefs about nature, "symbolic models" or "paradigms" (patterns) that underlie and inform the development of understanding. Scientific dilemmas are often resolved through creative or irrational processes, even by the symbolism of dreams experienced by the scientific researcher. As science has evolved, so has its language – a shorthand of signs, symbols and formulae that enables scientists to formulate and communicate knowledge.

SCIENTIFIC PARADIGMS AND SYMBOLISM

New scientific eras come about through "paradigm shifts", characterized by a radical shift in the symbolic worldview that eventually shakes up and fundamentally reorganizes the technologies and social and economic structures of the day. When the pioneering chemist Antoine Laurent Lavoisier (1743–94) showed water to be a compound substance made up of different elements he was severely criticized, in particular by the pharmacist Antoine Baumé, for undermining scientific theories based upon the fundamental elements of fire, water, air and earth. Each change in scientific understanding is accompanied by doubts and resistance, and new paradigms inevitably involve radical shifts in the scientific foundations and belief systems of a civilization.

THE SCIENTIFIC REVOLUTION

In the medieval universe, Heaven and earth were seen as two separate realms. Heaven centred on God and was governed by eternal law, while earth and humanity were governed by natural law. Though Heaven was hierarchically superior, earth was considered to be the centre of the universe.

This worldview was overturned by the scientific revolution of the 16th century, which, challenged by the astronomy of Copernicus and observations made with Galileo's telescope, supported the view of a much larger universe centred on the sun, seriously challenging statements made in the Old Testament. The Catholic Church fought back but a new worldview emerged that symbolically removed both humanity and the earth from the centre of things.

THE MACHINE

The French philosopher René Descartes (1596–1650) was a key figure in the transition from medieval to modern scientific thought, proposing an analytic method of searching for scientific truth and accepting only things that are beyond doubt. In the Cartesian era, scientific enquiry favoured mechanistic values of quantity and function over the qualitative values of spirit, aesthetics, feelings, the senses and nature itself, and the machine became a central metaphor.

The steam engine, developed during the 17th and 18th centuries, paved the way for the invention of industrial processes, leading to mass production. The machine became a symbol of power, organization and human control over nature.

THE QUANTUM ERA

During the 20th century a radically new scientific perspective began to emerge, introducing a worldview of tendencies and interdependence: both observer and observed exist in a quantum entanglement, whereby the very act of observation affects the thing being observed. The physicist Werner Heisenberg (1901–76) stated that when we attempt to look objectively at nature and the universe we really encounter ourselves, suggesting that science has an inner and archetypal origin. To explore the relationship between archetypal symbolism and scientific concepts the scientist Wolfgang Pauli (1900–58) examined the deep

RIGHT Galileo's heliocentric universe challenged the symbolic importance of the earth, and he was forced to recant by the Vatican.

archetypal dreams he was experiencing, and he hypothesized a psychophysical unity, which Jung called the *unus mundus*, or "world soul".

DREAMS, SYMBOLISM AND SCIENTIFIC DISCOVERY

What is the connection between symbolism and scientific models? Science itself is not simply a rational process, as there are many examples of scientific discoveries being made through dreams and other irrational processes – such as the Newtonian legend that an apple falling upon Sir Isaac Newton's head led him to an understanding of the force of gravity. It seems that the unconscious can produce symbols that may inform the next step in scientific exploration.

The most famous example is the discovery of the benzene ring in 1865 by the German chemist Friedrich August Kekulé. The properties of benzene could not be explained in terms of linear molecular structures. One evening, dozing in front of the fire, Kekulé dreamed of long rows of atoms "winding and turning like serpents" until one of these serpents caught hold of its tail. On awakening he hypothesized the ring-like structure of benzene, leading to a prolific new period in the development of organic chemistry. At a convention in 1890 Kekulé advised his fellow scientists to "learn to dream" in order to seek the truth.

Also in the mid-19th century, a Russian chemist, Dmitri Mendeleev, dreamed the periodic table of the elements with remarkable accuracy, even predicting the existence of three previously "non-existent" elements, all of which were discovered within 15 years. In the early 20th century, the Danish physicist Niels Bohr, studying the structure of the atom, saw in a dream a nucleus with electrons spinning around it, and for his subsequent work received the Nobel Prize for Physics in 1922. Albert Einstein credited the source of his theory of relativity to a dream he had while at school, in which he rode upon a sled that accelerated to an incredible degree, transforming the stars around him into dazzling light as he approached the speed of light.

SCIENTIFIC SIGNS

In order to communicate, formulate and develop scientific knowledge, a shorthand language of scientific symbols and signs has evolved. The sciences of astronomy, botany, biology, chemistry, nuclear chemistry, physics, geology, mathematics and meteorology have each developed their own shorthand.

The earliest chemical symbols were used by the ancient Greeks, and adopted by Plato, to represent the properties of the four elements: earth, air, fire and water. The alchemists introduced a symbolic language – drawn from astronomy, astrology, cosmology and metallurgy – to depict various elements, including the seven metals. Copper was associated with the element earth. Gold, representing the perfection of matter, was symbolized by the sun. Mercury (or quicksilver), a liquid metal that transcended earth and Heaven, and life and death, was linked with the astrological planet of the same name, or the serpent. Silver was associated with the moon and tin with the planet Jupiter. Iron was represented by the symbol for the planet Mars and lead by that for the planet Saturn.

American astronomers use the symbol of a dashed circle to represent a group of galaxies, while a circle leaning to the right depicts a single galaxy.

MATHEMATICAL SIGNS

In mathematics two parallel lines together mean the same as or equal to (in the same dimension), while a group of three parallel lines shows an equivalence or similarity in identity where there is no real difference. Interestingly this same symbol in meteorology refers to mist, an atmospheric pattern in which everything looks milky-white and loses its identity.

The plus sign (which may have originated as an abbreviated form of the Latin word *et*, meaning "and") came into common use in the 16th century to denote addition. Signs for multiplication and division were introduced in the 17th century.

RIGHT, FROM TOP TO BOTTOM The alchemical signs for copper, gold, silver, mercury, tin, iron and lead.

DIRECTORY OF SIGNS

From early cave drawings to contemporary logos, graphic symbols have been used to carry ideas, concepts and meaning. The following pages contain over 1000 ideograms, graphic motifs, symbols and line drawings. Each sign or symbol has a brief explanation of its meaning or use. Some of the most primitive symbols have multiple meanings, or meanings that have now been lost or superceded, others, like the spiral, have a universal consistent meaning. Many of the signs in these pages are talked about in more depth in other sections of the book. Signs such as the cross or alchemical symbols such as mercury, have an astonishing number of variations, and many of these are included to show the fascinating diversity of the symbols human society uses to convey both the tangible and the abstract.

RIGHT Cave paintings of the human hand have been found in South Africa, South America and Australia. Did the hands have the same poignancy to those who painted them, were they meant as signatures? We will never know, but it is universal signs like this that weave a continuous fabric of communication throughout our cultures.

A The first letter of the alphabet, used to signify the best, first.

ACTIVE INTELLECT Unknown origin, also one of the signs for water.

ADINKRAHENE Most important of the Ghanaian adinkra symbols, signifying the importance of playing a leading role.

ADONI Hebrew word meaning a lord who is not God.

AEROPLANE Spiritual aspiration, and the transcendence of human limitations.

AIR The element. Kabbalistic sign.

AIR The element. Old chemistry symbol.

AKOBEN Ghanaian adinkra symbol meaning vigilance and wariness. The akoben is a horn used to sound a battle cry.

AKOKONAN "Leg of the hen", Ghanaian adinkra symbol meaning mercy, nurturing. Inspired by the hen's habit of treading on her chicks without hurting them, being a protective but also corrective parent.

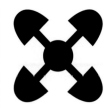

AKOMA NTOSO Ghanaian adinkra symbol meaning understanding and agreement.

ALCHEMY, the art of. The sun sign is at the centre, surrounded by the four elemental triangles, crowned with the Christian cross, and then placed in a circle representing the eternal or spiritual dimension.

ALCHEMY, the art of, variation. Used in the 17th century, this sign was created under the influence of Pythagorean geometry mysticism.

ALCHEMY, the art of, variation. This symbol is also engraved on rock faces dating from 1000 BC in Uxmal,

Central America. The symbol was adopted by Rudolf Steiner and is associated with Steiner's anthroposophy.

ALCOHOL Alchemistic sign.

ALCOHOL Early chemical sign.

ALEMBIC Alchemistic sign for distillation flask or still. Also used in early chemistry.

ALGOL The fixed star, used in some Kabbalistic mysticist contexts on magical amulet seals.

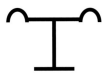

ALGORAB The fixed star, used in Kabbalistic magical amulet seals.

ALINEA Typographical sign used in printed texts, meaning the beginning of a new train of thought.

ALL IS WELL Ground to air emergency code.

ALMOND An important symbol with pagan and Christian roots associated with purity and virgin birth. Its juice was associated with semen in the ancient world. Biblical tradition says that Aaron's priestly status was shown by his rod blossoming and producing almonds. Western art often shows Mary and Jesus enclosed in an almond-shaped aureole.

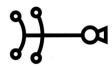

ALPHA The first letter of the Greek alphabet, associated with beginnings. Linked with God, who is said to be the alpha and omega – the beginning and the end. Also once a secret sign of the Christian faith.

ALPHECCA The fixed star, used as a Kabbalistic magical amulet seal.

ALUM Alchemistic sign.

AMALGAM Alchemistic sign.

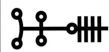

AMALGAMATION Alchemistic sign.

traditions, heavenly creatures in Jewish, Christian and Islamic traditions, thought to be evolved from Semitic and Egyptian winged deities. Seen as messengers, warriors, guardians or protectors.

ANT Hard work, organized community. The anthill is a symbol of industrious life in Tibetan Buddhism; in parts of Africa it is associated with fertility and creativity.

ANTI-CLOCKWISE SPIRAL Dynamic symbol of life force, cosmic and earthly.

APHRODITE Sign of the goddess.

APRICOT In China, the apricot is a symbol for a beautiful woman; the Japanese plum (*ume*) is sometimes called an apricot.

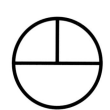

AMPERSAND Typographical sign meaning "and".

ANIMALIA The animal kingdom, 18th century.

ANTARES The fixed star, Kabbalistic magical amulet seal.

ANTIMONY Alchemistic, also used in medicine.

APOLLO This symbol of the god is based on the shape of the lyre, which was Apollo's instrument.

AQUA REGIA Alchemistic sign for "king's water".

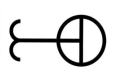

ANARCHISM Synonym for the political movement.

ANKH A cross topped with a loop; ancient Egyptian symbol of immortal life. Later adopted as a Christian symbol by the Egyptian Coptic Church.

ANTELOPE In Africa associated with the moon and fecundity; for the Bambara (Mali) the animal was sent by the creator god to teach humans agriculture.

ANVIL In Polynesia and parts of Africa, associated with the female principle and fertility; in Scottish folklore, linked with magical powers of the blacksmith.

APPLE Symbol of bliss, especially sexual; emblem of love, marriage, spring, youth, fertility and immortality. Linked with the forbidden fruit of the Garden of Eden and so a Christian symbol of temptation and original sin.

AQUA REGIA Alchemistic sign for king's water, variation.

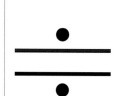
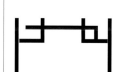

ANCHOR In early Christianity, a secret sign for the cross; hope, salvation. Also a symbol of the sea; of steadfastness and safety; and of the self.

ANSUR Rune for A

ANTI NUCLEAR CAMPAIGN The emblem of the Campaign for Nuclear Disarmament, made up of the semaphore signs for the letters "N" and "D".

APE Respected in ancient Egypt, Africa, India and China, but distrusted in the Christian tradition, where it is a symbol of vice and lust.

APPROXIMATELY EQUAL TO Mathematical sign.

AQUARIUS Zodiac sign.

ANGEL Symbol of divine will in several

ARATHRON Planet, mystical Kabbalistic sign for the first Olympic spirit.

ARCH Triumph and victory; grand human achievements.

ARCTURUS The fixed star, Kabbalistic magic amulet seal.

ARES Sign of the god.

ARES Sign of the god, variation.

ARES Sign of the god, variation.

ARIES Zodiac sign.

ARK OF THE COVENANT One of the symbols of the Jewish faith, a chest that was God's pledge of divine protection. The ark was kept in another symbol of Judaism, the Tabernacle.

ARK OR BOAT A symbol of salvation and preservation found in the mythology of peoples all around the world. In Christianity the ark stands for the Church, for Mary or for Christ; in secular symbolism it is a symbol of the Earth adrift in space.

ARM Symbol of power and strength; the many arms given to

Hindu gods symbolize their complexity and power. An upraised arm can suggest either a threat or a blessing. The arm also has protective connotations.

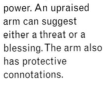

ARMOUR In medieval Europe, armour symbolized the knightly virtues of courage, protection, honour and strength; symbol of warrior class in China and Japan.

ARROW As directional sign.

ARROW/ARROW HEAD Penetration – by light, death, love or perception. Linked to sun symbols and the piercing darts of love.

ARROW, CURVED Ancient sign found in prehistoric cave art in Western Europe.

ARROW, WAVY Sea currents.

ARROW, WEAPON In Islam stands for the wrath of Allah, in Christianity for martyrdom and death. Bundled or broken in Native American symbolism, arrows stand for peace.

ARSENIC Alchemistic sign.

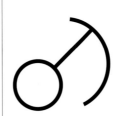

ARSENIC Alchemistic sign, variation.

ARSENIC Alchemistic sign, variation.

ARSENIC Alchemistic sign, variation.

ASS The god, later oss, rune for rapids or waterfall.

ASS See Donkey

ASTERISK Typographical sign for footnote.

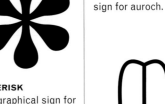

ATOM Also uranium, nuclear reactor (on maps), nuclear research, nuclear physics.

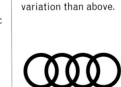

ATOM, less common variation than above.

AUDI Corporate emblem of the car manufacturers, symbol of unity and togetherness.

AUROCH The rune Ur, sign for auroch.

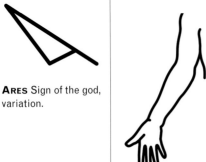

AUTUMN Old Germanic time sign.

AUTUMN Old Germanic time sign, variation.

AXE Almost universal symbol of decisive power and authority. Associated with the creative force of the thunderbolt. Linked with ancient sun and storm gods. Used to invoke thunder and rain in West Africa; symbol of the union of families in Chinese marriage.

BADGER Linked with playfulness in China; in Celtic tradition with slyness, deceit.

BALL Symbol of childhood games; in China, associated with the sun and the yin/yang symbol.

BAMBOO Chinese symbol of resilience, longevity, happiness

and spiritual truth; Japanese symbol of truth and devotion.

BANANA Freudian phallic symbol.

BASILISK A medieval symbol of lust and disease.

BASKET Womb symbol; in the Americas, stories about baskets and basket-making are related to women.

BASS CLEF Music notation.

BEANS Symbol of fecundity, used as love charms in India and to ward off evil spirits in Japan.

BEAR Emblem of masculine courage and primeval force; while she-bears symbolize care and warmth – although Jung linked them with dangerous aspects of the unconscious. In Christian and Islamic traditions the bear is cruel and lustful.

BAT Associated with death, symbol of fear and superstition, linked with witchcraft and the occult in Western folklore. In Africa and ancient Greece it was a symbol of perspicuity. Can signify madness. Underworld divinity in Central American and Brazilian mythology.

BATH Associated with bathing and thus with purification, both spiritual and physical.

BEE/BEEHIVE Society, industry and working together; honeybees are also linked with romantic love in European, Chinese and Hindu traditions. Bees are linked with death and the otherworld in European folklore.

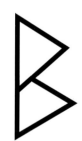

BELL The voice that proclaims the truth, especially in Buddhist, Hindu, Islamic and Christian traditions. In China it symbolizes obedience and cosmic harmony. Small tinkling bells can represent happiness and sexual pleasure. Worn on Hebrew dresses as a sign of virginity. Linked with the

BEARD Important aspect of male symbolism, representing dignity, sovereignty, virility and wisdom. Sign of a king; in ancient Egypt beardless rulers, including women, were depicted with false beards to proclaim their status.

feminine principle, also protective. Marks the passing of time and proclaims good news, warns of danger and tolls for death.

BELT OR GIRDLE Female chastity, marital fidelity or seductiveness. Magic girdles appear in myth as emblems of strength and became a symbol of honour in England. The rope girdles of monks allude to the scourging of Christ. The Hindu girdle is an emblem of the cycles of time.

BEORC Rune for B.

BETHOR The planet; mystical Kabbalistic sign for the second Olympic spirit.

BIOHAZARD Warning, USA.

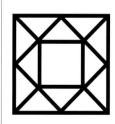

BIRCH Beneficial, protective, sacred to Germanic gods. Cosmic tree of Central Asia. In shamanic rites it symbolized human ascent to the spirit world.

BIRDS Symbol of the human soul, representing goodness and joy, standing for wisdom, intelligence and the swift power of thought. Aboriginal stories suggest they bear information. In Western art birds can symbolize air and touch.

BIRTH CHART Elizabethan England, 17th century.

BISON/BUFFALO
High-status animal in India and South-east Asia. In China the domestic buffalo is associated with the contemplative life. For North American Indians it symbolizes strength, prosperity, plenty and supernatural power.

BJARKAN Rune associated with new life and growth.

BLESSED SIGN One of the blessed signs that appears, among other places, in the early symbolism of the Buddha's footprints in India. In the West this symbol stands for the hexachord, and for harmonics in general.

BLESSING/HARMLESS
A variation of the pope's cross.

BLINDFOLD/BLIND
Spiritual blindness; in Masonic ritual, removing the blindfold symbolizes spiritual illumination. In classical antiquity, Fortuna (goddess of fortune) is blindfolded to show that she favours none above any other.

BMW Corporate emblem of the car manufacturer, a variation of the sun cross, the ancient structure for the sun's energy.

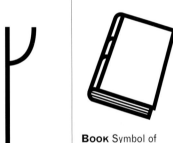

BOAR Primordial symbol of strength, aggression and resolute courage

across the northern and the Celtic worlds. Sacred as a sun symbol in Iran, and a moon symbol in Japan. It became a Christian symbol for tyranny and lust.

BOAT Symbol of womb-like protection, also linked to the salvation and regeneration symbolism of the ark.

BOIL/ABCESS
Alchemical sign.

BOIL (verb). Old Germanic.

BOIL (verb). Alchemistic sign.

BONES Symbol of possible reincarnation or bodily resurrection for ancient societies. Ancient beliefs held that the essence of a person was contained in the bones, a connection that is echoed in the phrase "felt in the bones".

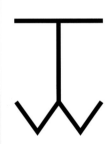

BOOK Symbol of knowledge and wisdom in many sacred traditions (Judaic, Christian, Islam); in ancient Egypt, the Book of the Dead was a collection of sacred charms buried with the dead to assist them in the afterlife.

BORAX Alchemistic sign.

BORAX/TINKAL
Alchemistic sign.

BOW Symbol of stored energy, willpower, aspiration, love, divine power and tension. Emblem of war and hunting. In Oriental thought it also represented spiritual discipline.

BOWL/VESSEL
Alchemistic.

BOX Symbol of womb and female unconscious, associated with secrets and hiding. In classical myth, Pandora's box is a symbol of what must not be opened.

BRACELET As jewellery can denote rank. May also be used as identity tags.

BRASS Alchemistic.

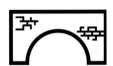

BREAD A staple of life, associated with hope in the Hebrew tradition, unleavened bread symbolizes purification and sacrifice. Christian metaphor for the food of the spirit, and the body of Christ.

BRIDGE Spans two distinct realms (Heaven and Earth, matter and spirit, the visible and the invisible); transition symbol, the crossing of one state to another.

BRIDLE In classical antiquity, said to have been invented by Athena, goddess of peace and war; associated with temperance and restraint, as in "bridling" or the reining in of passions.

BROOM Associated with magical powers from ancient times. A symbol of removal. Western folklore links brooms with witches due to the belief that evil spirits could bewitch the implement used to drive them out.

BUBBLE Symbol of illusion (Buddhism, Taoism); the transient and ephemeral.

BUCKLE OF ISIS Ancient Egyptian protection sign.

BUDDHA The seated Buddha is a symbol of enlightenment.

BUFFALO See Bison

BULL Hugely symbolic animal representing moon, sun, earth, sky, rain, heat, feminine procreation, male ardour, matriarch and patriarch, death, regeneration. In cave art the bull is a symbol of vital energy. The bull's bellowing stamping energy is linked with thunder and earthquakes, especially in Crete.

BULL ROARER Musical instrument and cult object common to indigenous peoples (Americas, Australia); when whirled in the air, it makes an otherworldly roaring sound, similar to the sound of thunder. Used in shamanic ritual and initiation ceremonies to communicate with the spirit world and with the ancestors.

BULL'S HORNS Linked with the crescent moon.

BUTTERFLY Symbol of the soul and resurrection as far apart as Congo, Mexico and Polynesia. Also a symbol of life and its cycle; in Western art Christ is sometimes depicted as holding a butterfly.

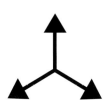

CADUCEUS The staff of the snake, the attribute of the Greek god Hermes, and the Roman equivalent Mercury, symbolizes the mediation between opposing forces and has been interpreted as an emblem of homeopathic medicine. The caduceus is also a symbol of commerce.

CALCINATIONS Alchemistic sign.

CALF Associated with feasting, hospitality and celebration (as in "the fatted calf") and also with sacrifice (Judaism).

CALTRAP Heraldic device, originally spiked objects used in battle to bring down cavalry horses.

CAMEL Traditional symbol of wealth and status in the Middle East; in medieval Europe a symbol of temperance; in Christianity the camel is associated with humility and obedience.

CAMELLIA A Chinese symbol of health and fortitude. Associated in Japan with sudden death.

CANCER Zodiac sign.

CANCER Zodiac sign, variation.

CANDLE A symbol of spiritual illumination, witness and joy. Its short-lived flame is a metaphor for the solitary, aspiring human soul.

CANNABIS LEAF Symbol of Rastafarianism, whose followers believe it is a "holy herb" whose use is grounded in scripture; a symbol of protest against white mainstream society; also a symbol of youth culture in Western society.

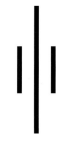

CANNON/GUN Also iron in early chemistry.

CANOPY Shade and protection, also associated with royal power, symbol of heavenly protection.

CAPRICORN Zodiac sign.

CAPRICORN Zodiac sign, variation.

CAPRICORN Zodiac sign, variation.

CAPRICORN Zodiac sign, variation.

CARDS, PLAYING Associated with gaming, gambling and fortune-telling in Europe and Asia. The cards themselves contain symbolic imagery (the court cards, joker, the four suits) and numbers.

CARP In China an emblem of longevity, virility and scholarly success. Images of carp were used on ship's masts or roofs to ward off fire.

CARPET/RUG Sacred and secular use in the Middle East; used to mark and beautify holy and domestic spaces. In Europe, carpets have symbolized status, with a red carpet having ritual use in public ceremonies involving high-ranking dignitaries, royalty and celebrities.

CASTLE/FORTRESS Archetypal symbol of protection and a place of refuge (spiritual and temporal); a place that is set apart and hard to enter, containing the heart's desire.

CAT Symbol of transformation, clairvoyance, agility, watchfulness, sensual beauty, mystery and female malice. In Rome seen as emblem of liberty. Their nocturnal habits and powers of transformation were distrusted.

CAT, BLACK Linked with evil cunning in the Celtic world, with harmful djins in Islam and with bad luck in Japan. Associated irrevocably with witchcraft and the Devil in the west.

CATERPILLAR In India, a symbol of the transmigration of souls; for the ancient Romans, it was an emblem of greed and ugliness.

CAULDRON Linked with magic, symbol of transformation, germination, plenty, and the possibility of rebirth or rejuvenation. Also linked with torture, trial or punishment.

CAVE Most primal symbol of shelter, linked with the womb, birth, rebirth, origin and the centre. Darker meanings include the entrance to Hell or the unconscious.

CELTIC KNOT Symbol of the universe, because it was drawn in a continuous line, and therefore used as a protective sign.

CAVE Very old ideogram for cave, farm, village or fortress, also used on modern maps for cave.

CEDAR Symbol of power and immortality.

CELTIC HARP Symbol of the bardic tradition, but also has links with the underworld. Used as a symbol for Ireland.

CENTAUR A mythical hybrid creature, half man and half horse, became a symbol of duality, of man trapped by his physical or sensual impulses, especially lust and violence.

CERBERUS Guardian of the entrance to the Greek underworld, symbol of the fearful uncertainties of death.

CERES Asteroid.

CHAI The Hebrew word for "life", commonly used on necklaces and other ornaments.

CHAIN A symbol of attachment and connection, the relationship between two things. Gold chains signify honour and status. A modern symbol of slavery and captivity. Broken chains symbolize the fight for freedom, and the achievement of liberty from oppression.

CHAIR Universal symbol of authority and superior rank, linked to the throne. Among the Swahili (Zanzibar) the "chair of power" is for visitors and the most important members of the family.

CHALICE/CUP A vessel of plenty and also of immortality; in Christianity, the chalice is a ritual cup used at Eucharist; in Medieval Europe, this cup was associated with the Holy Grail. In Japan, exchanging cups is a symbol of faithfulness and forms part of the marriage ceremony.

CHARIOT A dynamic symbol of rulership in ancient iconography; a symbol of spiritual authority and the mastery of gods and heroes. Hindu mysticism associates charioteering as a symbol of the Self, and in moral allegory it is an image of the triumphant journey of the spirit.

CHER Rune for harvest. Also known as Jara.

CHERRY A Samurai emblem in Japan, the fruit is a symbol of virginity in China, and its blossom is highly auspicious. In Christian iconography the cherry is an alternative to the apple as the fruit of paradise.

CHERUB A type of angelic being in Islamic, Judaic and Christian traditions; in Christian art cherubim are shown as winged children representing innocence, with blue wings that symbolize the sky.

CHEVRON A symbol of rank in military and heraldic contexts.

CHEVRON A heraldic variation.

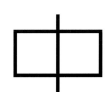

CHICKEN In parts of South America (Makumba cult), the Caribbean (Voodoo) and Africa, a cult animal; a guide of souls in initiation rites, sacrificial animal. Tenth sign of the Chinese zodiac.

CHILDBIRTH Child is born, genealogy.

CHIMERA A mythological snake-lion-goat hybrid creature, symbol of the victory of spirit over matter.

CHIMNEY A phallic symbol in Freudian psychology.

CHINA Used from the earliest Chinese writings as a symbol of how they viewed their civilization, as the "empire of the Middle", set between Heaven and Earth, and in the centre of an otherwise uncivilized world.

CHRIST A monogram formed by the initials of Christ in their Greek form, PX. In this variation the X is turned 45 degrees to form a cross.

CHRIST Monogram, variation.

CHRIST Monogram, variation.

CHRIST Monogram, variation.

CHRIST Monogram, variation.

CHRIST Another monogram symbolizing Christ, this one is built up by

CHRIST Monogram, variation, combined with the Greek letters alpha and (lower case) omega, the first and last letters of the Greek alphabet to symbolize Christ as first and last.

CHRIST Monogram, variation, the triangle at the base is a symbol of divinity meaning that Christ is the centre of the Holy Trinity.

CHRIST Monogram, variation.

a cross above the letters alpha and omega, signifying that Christ is the first and the last.

CHRONOS God.

CHRONOS God, variation.

CHRONOS God, variation.

CHRYSANTHEMUM A solar and imperial symbol in Japan, linked with longevity and joy; a Chinese Taoist symbol; and in Western art it is used as a symbol of autumn.

CHRYSLER Corporate emblem of the car manufacturer, a variation of the pentagon combined with the pentagram.

CHURCH In Christianity an image of the world; also associated with the Bride of Christ and the Mother of Christians, and therefore with motherhood.

CINNABAR Alchemistic sign.

CIRCLE Intersected with diagonal cross, modern sign for zero position on machines.

CIRCLE Intersected with diagonal line, Greek letter phi, commonly used in computer programs for zero. In other contexts it signifies diameter or average number.

CIRCLE Intersected with horizontal line, another of humankind's earliest ideograms, found on rock paintings in the inner Sahara and many early systems of writing. Used in modern contexts to mean open. On ships it is the main part of the plimsoll mark.

CIRCLE Intersected with upright cross, a rare sign sometimes used in alchemy for oil or wax. In musical notation it signifies "to be repeated".

CIRCLE AND ARROW One of the most common ideograms in Western culture. Sign for the planet Mars. Also for iron and zinc, and morning.

CIRCLE On horizontal line, ancient ideogram perhaps signifying greatness and power.

CIRCLE On several decreasing horizontal lines, meaning unknown; appears in several prehistoric European caves.

CIRCLE On vertical line, ancient ideogram; in ancient Greece it was a sign for Aphrodite; in alchemy a sign for night.

CIRCLE With vertical line continuing downwards, one of the oldest ideograms, it also appeared in the runic alphabet where for a while it stood for the m-sound.

CIRCLE Divided by horizontal line, often found on rock carvings. In early Chinese calligraphy it denoted the sun; in the Greek alphabet it is the letter theta.

CIRCLE Divided by vertical line, an ancient sign in early alphabets from the Near East. Alchemistic sign for nitrogen.

CIRCLE Empty, one of the oldest ideograms. Sometimes represents the sun or the moon, and also openings such as eyes or the mouth. Used in ideographic writing for up to 5000 years.

CIRCLE Filled, perhaps the most common of the ancient ideograms found in many ancient cultures.

CIRCLE Semi, on vertical line, iconic sign for rising sun, used for dew in meteorology.

CIRCLE Another very early ideogram, associated with the divine or powerful. In Buddhist and Christian art it is used to denote charisma or halo.

CIRCLES Small, connected by straight lines, very old structure found in ancient China and in Nordic rock carvings. In Kabbalistic mystical contexts, similar signs are used for stars and sounds.

CIRCLES Three, filled, known as bowl hollows, these have been found in Nordic rock carvings; also used in modern maps to indicate ruins or sights worth seeing. Used in meteorology for rain. In mathematics and geometry it means therefore. Used upside down, the sign means because.

CITROËN Corporate emblem of the car manufacturer, inspired by the V symbol for victory and military superiority.

CLAY Alchemistic sign.

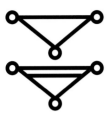

CLOAK Its symbolism of metamorphosis and concealment is due to the instant change it makes to the wearer's appearance. In Teutonic and Celtic legends, magic cloaks are associated with invisibility and forgetfulness. The cloak also symbolizes intrigue, and the world of espionage.

CLOCK Symbol of time and of the transience of life; a stopped clock can symbolize death, and in South America they are placed on graves to symbolize the transition between life and death.

CLOUD Symbol of fecundity and revelation; in China pink clouds are signs of happiness. Cloud nine is mystical bliss. Modern associations are with gloom, obscurity or depression.

CLOVES Represent health and sweetness in Japan and China; in Japanese art, they were one of the Myriad Treasures carried by the Seven Deities of Good Fortune.

CLUB Has a dual role representing either primitive brutality or heroism in art.

CLUBS Suit of playing cards.

COAGULATE/FIX Alchemistic sign.

COBRA. In India cobra divinities, (nagas) were guardian symbols, generally benevolent. The Hindu cobra has a jewel in its hood and symbolizes spiritual treasure. The erect, hooded cobra is the protective serpent emblem of royal power, used by the pharaohs as an emblem to strike down enemies. There is a general link between snakes and wisdom or prophecy.

COBRA On ancient Egyptian headdresses the cobra was a protective sign and a symbol of royal power.

COCK Generally positive symbolic links with the dawn, the sun and illumination. In China the cock was a funerary emblem warding off evil. In Japan it is a sacred creature. In Islam the cock was seen by Mohammed in the First Heaven. Cocks also symbolize lust.

COCONUT Extensive use in Hindu rituals; "sacrificed" as a replica for the human head and is also associated with Shiva, because its three "eyes" symbolize the eyes of Shiva. Also associated with fertility.

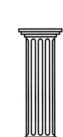

COLUMN/PILLAR Symbols of temporal and spiritual aspiration and power; God appeared to the Israelites in the wilderness as a pillar of fire. Two columns appear outside Masonic temples, representing force and form.

COMB Sacred and protected in Maori tradition.

COMET A change in the heavens; in many cultures a portent of war and disaster. Also a symbol of hope and new beginnings.

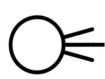

COMET Variation.

COMET Variation.

COMPASSES Associated with architecture during the Renaissance; in European art it can

symbolize the rational mind. Together with the set square it is one of the most important symbols of Freemasonry.

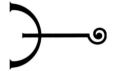

COMPOSE Alchemistic sign.

CONCH SHELL Buddhists, the Maya and the Aztecs used the conch as a ceremonial horn. Its shape associates it with the symbolism of the spiral. In Hinduism the sound of the conch symbolizes the origin of existence. An emblem of Vishnu.

CONDOR A solar symbol in South America.

CONFERENCE Modern sign, similar to older signs meaning togetherness.

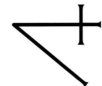

CONFUSED MENTAL STATE Used in modern comic strips.

CONSTELLATIONS OF FIXED STARS Chinese.

COPYRIGHT SYMBOL Used to denote lawful ownership of text or images.

CORAL Its red colour links it with blood in many traditions: for Christians it symbolizes Christ's Passion; in Greek myth, it was formed from the drops of Medusa's blood. In ancient Rome, coral necklaces were worn to ward off disease.

CORN In European cultures, associated with summer, harvest and fertility.

CORNUCOPIA Roman horn of plenty that cannot be emptied; it is used to denote abundance and prosperity in Western art, and is a feminine symbol of maternal nourishment and love. Attribute of Dionysus, god of wine, Demeter and Priapus, also of the allegorical figures of Earth, Autumn, Hospitality, Peace, Fortune and Concord in Western art.

COSMIC TREE The "tree of life" reversed so that its roots draw spiritual strength from the sky.

COW Ancient symbol of maternal nourishment, often personified as mother earth, and the moon.

To Hindus and Buddhists the cow's quiet, patient rhythms of life present a parallel with holiness.

COW Hindu, the symbolism of the cow is taken to its highest for Hindus, who view it as sacred. Its image everywhere is one of happiness.

COWRIE SHELL Symbol of wealth and rank in parts of Africa, appearing on costumes and artefacts; Freudian symbol for female sexual organs, also associated with fertility and good luck.

COYOTE A divinatory symbol or culture hero in North America and Africa.

CRADLE Womb symbol; associated with security, protection and safety. Its traditional boat-like shape also links it with travel; a symbol for a safe journey through life.

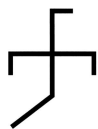

CRANE Linked by the Chinese to immortality; in Africa with the gift of speech, and widely with the ability to communicate with the gods. Christian symbolism sometimes links it with resurrection.

CRICKET Linked with death and resurrection in China; also a good luck symbol.

CROCODILE Major symbol of destructive voracity, bringer of divine punishment, and archetypal devourer. Treated with fearful respect as a creature of primordial and occult power over water, earth and the underworld. The ancient Egyptians had a crocodile fecundity god called Sebek. It has more positive connections in parts of Asia, where it appears as the inventor of the drum and of song.

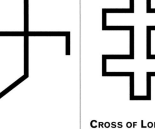

CROSS OF CHRIST.

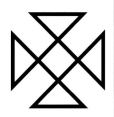

CROSS OF ENDLESSNESS A symbol for eternity.

CROSS OF GOLGOTHA Similar to the cross of the Crusaders.

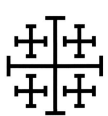

CROSS OF LAZARUS Ancient symbol for holiness and divinity.

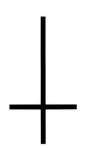

CROSS OF LORAINE Used in heraldry.

CROSS OF PALESTINE Used as a symbol for the kingdom of Jerusalem after the city was captured by the Crusaders.

CROSS OF PETER An upside-down Latin cross that commemorates the martyrdom of St Peter, who was crucified upside down.

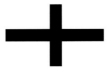
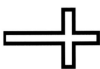
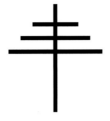
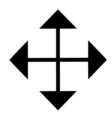

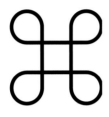
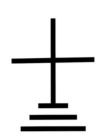

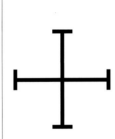

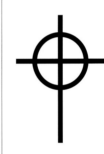

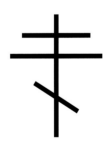

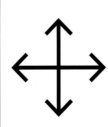

CROSS OF PHILIP Associated with Nordic countries, some of which use it in their flags.

CROSS OF ST ANDREW'S Named after the apostle Andrew, who was crucified on a diagonal cross.

CROSS OF ST ANTHONY Named after a hermit in Egypt, who was said to have chased away a pack of demons with a cross of this type. Also known as the Tau cross, T-cross, Egyptian cross, Crux commissa and the robber's cross.

CROSS OF ST BIRGITTA Set with five precious stones representing the five wounds of Christ.

CROSS OF ST GEORGE

CROSS OF ST HAN/ CROSS OF ST JOHN Also a magic ideogram from the Viking era, possibly also used in Kabbalism.

CROSS OF ST JOHN

CROSS OF THE ARCHANGELS Also known as the Golgata cross.

CROSS OF THE ARCHANGELS Variation.

CROSS OF THE EVANGELISTS

CROSS OF THE HOLY CHURCH Also used in alchemy for crucible.

CROSS OF THE PATRIARCH

CROSS OF THE POPE

CROSS OF THE ROBBERS

CROSS, ANCHORED One of the disguised crosses used by early Christians.

CROSS, ANGLED

CROSS, ARROWED Meaning expansion in all directions and for that reason a favoured symbol of fascists.

CROSS, ARROWED Variation.

CROSS, CELTIC

CROSS, CELTIC Variation.

CROSS, COPTIC

CROSS, DIAGONAL Equal-length arms, an extremely old sign found in prehistoric caves. Egyptian hieroglyph meaning divide, count. Signifies multiplication, confrontation, annulment, cancellation, opposition, obstruction, mistake and undecided.

CROSS, DISSIMULATA Variation of the disguised form of the cross used by early Christians.

CROSS, DISSIMULATA Variation, also used on the seal of the Prince of Byblos, a Phoenician city, in the year 2000 BC.

CROSS, EASTERN ORTHODOX

CROSS, EGYPTIAN/ COPTIC

CROSS With equal length arms, an old ideogram from most cultures found in every part of the world, often associated with the four elements. Used in mathematics as the sign for addition.

CROSS With filled or closed, short arms, common in ancient Greece, pre-Columbian America and the Near East up to 1000 years before the birth of Christ, associated with the sun and power.

CROSS, FITCHEE Originated in the times of the crusades when knights took crosses with them that could be thrust into the ground during worship in the field of battle or encampment.

CROSS, GREEK

CROSS, HOLY ROMAN Has a swastika in the centre, a possible allusion to the return of Christ.

CROSS, IRON/ MANTUAN CROSS Used as a German order medal.

CROSS, LABARUM/ CHI-RHO A monogram formed with the two initial Greek letters of the word Christ.

CROSS, LILY

CROSS, MALTESE Also known as the Cross of Promise. Used as the emblem of the Order of St John, based on old Assyrian symbols.

CROSS, MALTESE Variation.

CROSS Open with closed arms, an ancient symbol that seems to have been linked with the weather, the four winds or the four directions.

CROSS Sitting over a globe. Sign for world evangelization.

CROSS, PORTALE

CROSS, RESTORATION Used in the 15th century in heraldry and in European coinage. Also used by the Inca as a sign for sun.

CROSS, TAU/ EGYPTIAN

CROSS, TAU Variation with snake.

CROSS, SQUARE Representing the Earth with its four corners.

CROSS, WHEEL/SUN CROSS First appeared at the dawn of the Bronze Age, appearing in ancient Egypt, China, pre-Columbian America and the Near East. Associated with the wheel.

CROSS, WHEEL, DIAGONAL Suggests a cancelling or neutralizing characteristic.

CROSS, WITH GARMENT A symbol of the crucifixion.

CROSS, WITH ORB A symbol of the final triumph of Christ over the world.

CROSSROADS A symbol of decision-making, life changes and journeys.

CROW Emblem of war, death, solitude, evil and bad luck in Europe and India, but in the Americas and Australia has positive symbolism as a solar bird that is a creative, civilizing bird.

CROWN Identified with power, glory and consecration. Originating as wreaths, crowns draw on the celestial symbolism of the circle – representing perfection and the ring – representing continuity.

CROWN OF THORNS Originally mocking the symbolism of a crown (by the Roman soldiers who crucified Christ) it has now become a symbol in itself of sacrifice and consecration.

CROZIER Originated as a masculine fertility symbol, it implies royal or spiritual power to administer justice. Linked with the sceptre, the staff and the rod. One of the signs of a bishop's religious authority is his crozier.

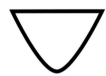

CRUCIBLE OR MELTING POT Alchemistic sign, also old chemistry.

CRUCIBLE Old chemistry, variation.

CRUX DISSIMULATA Christian symbol of hope.

CRYSTAL Modern New Age symbol.

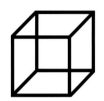

CUBE Linked to symbolism of the square, hence associated with the physical manifest world. A symbol of wisdom and perfection; for example in Freemasonry, ashlar (a smooth cube) represents the perfected person; one of Islam's most holy structures, the Ka'ba, is cube-shaped.

CUPID/EROS With his bow and arrows of desire, Cupid is a symbol of love and romance.

CURVED LINE A segment of a circle, appears in many ideographic systems, ancient and modern.

CYPRESS Western symbol of death and mourning, but in Asia and elsewhere a symbol of longevity and endurance.

DAEG Rune for D.

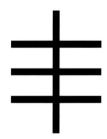

DAGGER/KNIFE Sacred symbol in Buddhist and Sikh religions. For Sikhs, it symbolizes courage and dignity. In Tibetan Buddhism a ritual dagger with a three-sided blade is used to protect sacred buildings. In European traditional lore, daggers are linked to treachery.

DAISY Christian symbol of innocence associated with the Virgin Mary, and the

rays of the sun; also sacred to Freya, the Germanic sky goddess.

DANGER Energy, the symbol for heat combined with an arrow.

DANGER Energy, heat, variation.

DANGER Poisonous, used in botany. Also stands for checkmate in chess.

DAY Rune associated with light, breakthrough and success.

DEATH The moment of/passing out, used in modern comic strips.

DECOCTION Alchemistic sign.

DEER Universally benevolent symbol associated with dawn, light, purity, regeneration, creativity and magic.

DENEB ALGEDI Magical amulet seal.

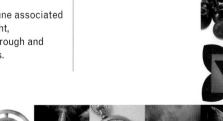

DENKYEM The crocodile, Ghanaian adinkra symbol meaning ability to adapt to circumstances, just as the crocodile adapts from water to land.

DISTAFF Used to prepare flax for spinning, a symbol of Athena/Minerva, Greco-Roman goddess of wisdom and inventor of spinning and weaving; also associated with the passing of time.

DIVINE POWER Ancient Nordic/Anglo Saxon sign; also logo for Mitsubishi Group.

DOG Symbol of loyalty; protective vigilance in Celtic and Christian traditions; in ancient thought associated with the underworld, where it acted as guide and guardian. Dogs are guardian symbols in Japan and China, but in China they also have demonic links.

heroes and carrier of souls to the Islands of the Blessed. Attribute of Poseidon, Aphrodite, Eros, Demeter and Dionysus. Entwined with an anchor, the dolphin can symbolize prudence.

good or evil forces to enter or leave, hence doorways are often guarded.

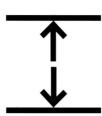

DHARMACHAKRA The Buddhist eight-spoked wheel.

DISTANCE Modern technical symbol.

DIVISION Mathematical sign.

DOSE OF MEDICINE Large pill or bolus, old pharmacology; also Japanese Buddhism, also in alchemy for orichalcum or dissolvent.

DIED IN BATTLE Military expression, also used on maps to denote a battle site.

DISTILLATION Alchemistic sign.

DIVISION Mathematical sign, variation.

DOLL Used in religion, ritual and magic as surrogates for people and deities.

DOME Symbol of the heavens, frequently appearing in sacred or important civic buildings, such as mosques, Byzantine churches or the Roman pantheon.

DOT, SINGLE One of the most common ancient Western ideograms in existence since the era of cave paintings and rock carvings.

DIGGING STICK Aboriginal, traditional tool used to gather roots and vegetables now used in modern art to represent ancestral being.

DISTILLED OIL Alchemistic sign.

DIVORCED Genealogy.

DOLLAR SIGN USA currency.

DONKEY/ASS Well-entrenched modern symbol of foolishness, but earlier connotations were much more positive (humility, poverty and patience), or sinister in both Egyptian and Indian mythology.

DOTS, THREE IN TRIANGLE Sign for therefore (modern).

DIVORCED Genealogy, variation.

DOLPHIN Widespread symbol of salvation, transformation and love. Emblem of Christ as saviour. In ancient Greek mythology the dolphin is the bearer of the gods, saviour of

DOOR/ENTRANCE A place of transition seen in many cultures as an opportunity for

DOTS IN A LINE Sign for something left out (modern). Several dots in a line was the sign for rain for the Anglo Saxons.

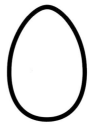

DOVE Universal symbol of peace, particularly when holding an olive branch – this is an allusion to the story of Noah, when the flood began to recede and land became visible. The dove is also a personification of the Holy Spirit and a symbol of baptism.

DOWN WITH! Sign of popular dissent, formed by the sign for "viva!" upside down.

DRAGON Benevolent symbol in the East, malevolent in the West, and containing a wealth of symbolism for each.

DRUM Primeval means of communication, symbol of creative power in India, the voice of Heaven in China, used to promote trance and ecstasy in shamanistic societies. In modern Western symbolism the drum is linked to war and warning.

DUCK Symbol of happiness in Japan and China, with a pair of mandarin ducks symbolizing marriage and domestic harmony.

DWELLING Egyptian hieroglyph.

Christian churches, usually on fonts, pulpits and lecterns, as one of the attributes of St John.

EAR Receptivity; in Africa, ears symbolize humans' animal nature. In the East, long earlobes are a symbol of wisdom and longevity. Ear piercing was traditionally an ancient sign of a pledge.

EARTH Element.

EARTH Element, Kabbalistic.

EAGLE An unambiguous and universal symbol of power, speed and perception. Attribute of the greatest gods, adopted much later as a symbol of imperial power. Also appears in carvings in

EARTH The planet, used as early as 500 BC. Used today on maps to signify a chapel. Alchemy sign for antinomy.

EARTH The planet, modern.

EARTH The planet, modern variation.

EARTH The planet, variation.

ECLIPSE OF THE MOON Astronomy.

EGG A universal symbol for creation, often the thing that life sprang from, whether vegetative, godly or elemental. A propitious symbol all over the world symbolizing luck, wealth, health, birth and resurrection. Also associated with spring. In Jewish tradition the egg is a symbol of promise.

EHWAZ Rune for E.

EIGHT Symbol of cosmic equilibrium and renewal. A lucky number in China.

EIGHTH HOUSE Astrology.

ELECTRICITY Thunder, lightning.

ELEPHANT Ancient symbol of sovereign power in India, China and Africa, and by this association linked with dignity, intelligence, prudence, peace. The mount of Indian rulers, and of the thunder and rain god, Indra. Ancient Rome associated the elephant with victory. Medieval Europe believed the male refrained from sex with its mate during her pregnancy, which made it an emblem of chastity, fidelity and love. The white elephant of Burma, Thailand and Cambodia is a symbol of fertility and rainfall.

ELEVENTH HOUSE Astrology.

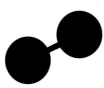

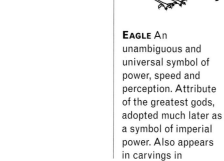

ELHAZ Rune for Z, meaning an elk.

ELLIPSIS Nothing, zero, absence.

EMPEDOCLES' ELEMENTS, AIR Pre-Socratian ancient Greek geometrical symbols of the elements.

EMPEDOCLES' ELEMENTS, EARTH Pre-Socratian ancient Greek geometrical symbols of the elements.

EMPEDOCLES' ELEMENTS, FIRE Pre-Socratian ancient Greek geometrical symbols of the elements.

EMPEDOCLES' ELEMENTS, WATER Pre-Socratian ancient Greek geometrical symbols of the elements.

EMPEROR Jesus, first, only one, self.

EMU Appears in Australian Aboriginal creation stories; therefore killing an emu is associated with bad luck.

ENCLOSED SPACE Tank or closed room, also buried in genealogy.

ENNEAGRAM Nine-pointed star, Christian, nine gifts of spirit.

ENTRANCE See Door

EOH Rune for Y, meaning yew tree.

EPA Ghanaian adinkra symbol, meaning handcuffs, symbol of slavery and captivity.

ERMINE Heraldry.

ESSENCE Alchemistic sign.

ETHERIC OIL Alchemistic sign.

EVAPORATION Modern.

EXCLAMATION MARK Modern, denoting surprise or emphasis in text.

EYE OF FIRE Ancient Germanic, four elements in alchemy.

EYE OF HORUS Symbol of cosmic wholeness, and of the all-seeing power of the ancient Egyptian god Horus. Also known as the wedjat.

EYE OF THE DRAGON Ancient Germanic sign for threat, danger.

EYE/EYEBROW The ability to see, vision (literal and metaphorical), associated with magic or spiritual power in many traditions. In Chinese Buddhism long eyebrows are a sign of wisdom and old age.

EYE, THE THIRD Also called the "eye of the heart", a symbol of the eye of spiritual perception in Hinduism, and of clairvoyance in Islam. Adopted by the Freemasons as one of their society's signs.

FAITH Early Christian symbol, one of those found inscribed in the catacombs where the Christians hid from Roman persecution. Fish are associated with hope in Hebrew tradition.

FALCON Identical symbolism to the hawk; a solar emblem of victory, superiority, aspiration, spirit, light and liberty. Many Egyptian gods are depicted with the head of a falcon. The eye of a falcon symbolizes sharp vision. In Western tradition the falcon is an emblem of the hunter, and in Nordic mythology of the sky god, Woden.

FAMILY A sign combining the sign for woman, the sign for man, and the sign for woman with child.

FAN Symbol of goodness (Chinese); an attribute of one of the Japanese Seven Deities of Good Fortune, and of Vishnu (Hindu god). Emblem of kingship in Africa, Asia and the Far East.

FASCES Pictorial representation of an axe wrapped around with rods and bound with leather, which Roman officials carried as a symbol of their authority. Later the fasces became a Roman punitive emblem of state power, and was later adopted by fascism.

FAST MOVEMENT Modern.

FE Rune, meaning cattle or livestock, also a Viking symbol for moveable property.

FEATHER Symbol of Maat, ancient Egyptian goddess of justice. In Native American traditions, feathers hold the spirit of the bird and are highly prized.

FEMALE

FEOH Rune for F.

FERN Koru fern, Polynesian.

FIAT Corporate emblem of the car manufacturer, derived from the sun cross.

FIFTH ELEMENT The quintessence or ether. The best.

FIFTH HOUSE Astrology.

FIG Symbol of fecundity, also in Buddhism of moral teaching and immortality.

FILTER (VERB) Alchemistic sign.

FINGERS/FINGERNAILS Connection with spiritual power (India), and with the five tenets of Islam. Long fingernails are traditionally a sign of wealth and status; long, claw-like nails are attributes of the kings of the Dahomey in Africa.

FIRE Very old ideogram, also used for lunar halo.

FIRE Masculine symbol of creation, destruction, purification, revelation, transformation, regeneration and spiritual or sexual ardour.

FIRE Alchemistic sign.

FIRE Kabbalism.

FIREPLACE See Hearth.

FIREWORK In the modern world associated with festivals and celebration, the more lavish the spectacle, the bigger the occasion; also associated with other symbolism, for example rocket, wheel, star, spiral.

FIRST HOUSE Astrology.

FISH Phallic symbol of sexual happiness and fecundity. In China the fish is an emblem of plenty and good luck. The letters of the Greek word for fish – *icthus* – form an acronym for Jesus Christ, and so the fish became an early secret Christian sign. In Hebrew tradition fish represent the true and faithful. Fish appear as saviours in Hindu myth.

FISH A simplified icon that was used by early Christians as the first emblem of Christ.

FISH HOOK Symbol of fishing and helpless entrapment.

FIVE ELEMENTS OF WESTERN IDEOGRAPHY, THE DOT Almost all Western ideography is based upon five basic shapes, the dot, the line, the semicircle and the two spirals.

FIVE ELEMENTS OF WESTERN IDEOGRAPHY, THE LINE

FIVE ELEMENTS OF WESTERN IDEOGRAPHY, THE SEMI-CIRCLE Also known as the section.

FIVE ELEMENTS OF WESTERN IDEOGRAPHY, THE SPIRAL Also depicted in reverse.

FIVE ELEMENTS OF WESTERN IDEOGRAPHY, THE SPIRAL Variation.

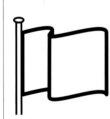

FIVE Associated with the human microcosm and the hand; important symbol of totality in China, Japan and Celtic tradition. Also associated with love, health, sensuality, meditation, analysis, criticism and the heart.

FIXATION Alchemistic.

FLAG Emblem of rulership and identity at many levels (international, national, local); in war, a symbol of military honour, with a white flag representing surrender; a fluttering flag can suggest new beginnings.

FLAMING HEART See Heart of fire.

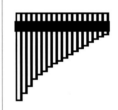

FLASK/BOTTLE Alchemistic sign for a flask that is not transparent.

FLASK Alchemistic sign for a flask made of glass.

FLEUR-DE-LYS A stylized lily with three flowers used as the emblem of France.

FLOW/MELT Alchemistic sign.

FLOWER Culmination or crowning achievement; feminine beauty; also a sign of impermanence and transience. Specific flowers also have their own symbolism, and, in some cultures, language. Widespread use in rituals all over the world (birth, marriage, death, celebrations).

FLUTE/PAN PIPES Associated with Pan (Greek god of the woods and fields), hence linked with nature and sexuality; bamboo flutes are associated with Zen Buddhist monks.

FLY Associated with sickness, death and the devil in many traditions.

FLY WHISK Symbol of royalty in many cultures, in Polynesia a mark of rank, for Buddhists a sign of compassion.

FOOT Bare feet are often a sign of humility. In the East, foot washing is an act of hospitality and a sign of love; Christ washing the feet of his disciples was a symbolic gesture of his love and service.

FOUNTAIN A source of water and therefore of life. Drinking from a fountain can symbolize spiritual refreshment or immortality. In Islamic tradition fountains represent the connection between humans and God.

FOUR ELEMENTS Medieval.

FOUR EVANGELISTS

FOUR EVANGELISTS Variation.

FOUR Solidity, organization, power, intellect, justice and omnipotence.

FOURTH HOUSE Astrology.

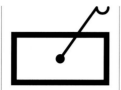

Fox In European traditions, associated with cunning and slyness, appearing in medieval art as a symbol of the devil. In China and Japan the fox is a bringer of wealth.

Frog Foetal symbol especially in Egypt, associated with magic, germination, evolution, the moon's phases, water and rain. Good luck emblem in Japan.

Fu Authority, Chinese.

Fulfoot Swedish variation of the swastika.

Fumes Alchemistic.

Funtunfunefu The Ghanaian adinkra symbol of Siamese crocodiles, who share one stomach but still fight over food. A warning against infighting and tribal conflict.

Gargoyle A carved waterspout, typically seen on the gutters of church or cathedral parapets. During the Middle Ages gargoyles were mostly grotesque or demonic, symbolizing the power of the Church to wash away evil.

Garlic Associated with strength and protection from evil spirits in many traditions. In antiquity garlic was associated with the moon and magic and was regarded as a powerful aphrodisiac.

Fumes Alchemistic.

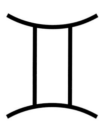

Gate A transitional symbol marking the movement from one place, time, spiritual or psychological state to another. Gates can also symbolize spiritual and/or secular power.

Gemini Zodiac sign.

Geofu Rune for G.

Giants An ancient ideogram probably first drawn 10,000 years ago, used in the Nordic runic alphabet as a sign for giants or Titans. Also used as an expression of power.

Glass/arsenic Alchemistic sign, also unmarried in genealogy.

Globe/orb Power emblem of gods or imperial rulers, symbol of totality.

Glove Powerful symbol of rank used as an acknowledgement of superiority or fealty, also as a love pledge.

Goat Ambiguous symbol meaning virility, lust, cunning and destructiveness in the male, and fecundity and nourishment in the female. Sign for Capricorn, one of the signs of the zodiac. In Roman myth the cornucopia derives from the horn of the goat, Amaltheia, the revered wet-nurse of the baby Zeus.

Goddess Of morning or evening, Greek and Byzantium.

Goddess

Gohei Sacred wands topped with zigzag streamers of white paper used in Shinto rituals.

Gold leaf/gold foil, Alchemistic sign.

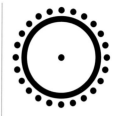

Gold Alchemistic, variation.

Gold Alchemistic, variation.

Gold Alchemistic, variation.

Golden number 17 From the medieval clog almanacs for calculating the phases of the moon.

Golden number 18 From the medieval clog almanacs for calculating the phases of the moon.

GONG Widespread use in sacred rituals in China and Japan. In Chinese temples they are beaten to gain the attention of the spirits, while Zen Buddhists use gongs as part of liturgical chanting and meditation. Sounding a gong can indicate arrivals or departures.

GOOSE Medieval bestiaries compared geese to the devout, although white geese were linked to fancy dressing and malicious gossip. The domestic goose is a symbol of the home, women, fidelity and married life. The wild goose is associated with cooperation, interdependence and vigilance. Because wild geese are said to stay with a sick goose, they are also symbols of loyalty.

GORGONS Snake-haired mythological winged women-hybrids of ancient Greece, embodiments of adversarial evil.

GOURD/CALABASH Pre-eminent symbol for many traditional African societies, where it appears in creation myths, representing the world egg or the womb.

GRAIL In European traditions the grail is a sacred object (typically a chalice or stone) whose wondrous powers confer the elixir of life and eternal youth; in medieval legend, particularly linked with King Arthur and his knights, it was believed to be the cup used by Christ at the Last Supper and used to catch his blood at the crucifixion.

GRAIN A central symbol of growth, rebirth and fertility, together with rice, corn, barley and wheat. Often an attribute of earth gods and goddesses. Ancient fertility symbol, used at weddings to sprinkle over the married couple.

GRAPES Complex ancient symbol of natural fecundity and of spiritual life in both pagan and Christian traditions.

GRASS The victory over barrenness, a fertile land; as a dream symbol, can represent new growth, new ideas and new enterprises.

GRAVE Related literally and symbolically to a place of residence for the dead and where the dead can be remembered. As a barrow or tumulus, it may be a symbolic allusion to holy mountains.

GRAVEL/SAND Alchemistic sign.

GRIFFIN Lion-eagle hybrid symbol of dominion over land and sky, evolved from an aggressive emblem of power into a protective symbol.

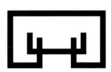

GRIND/CRUSH Alchemistic sign.

GROWING Also rebirth and genesis, Egyptian hieroglyphs for woman and female sex.

GYE NYAME Ubiquitous Ghanaian adinkra symbol, meaning "except for God", which is by far the most popular for use in decoration.

HAGALL Rune for H.

HAGITH Kabbalism.

HAIL Rune associated with accidents and misfortune.

HAIR A complex symbol with many meanings, most associated with the life force; can be a sign of holiness and strength, royal power, freedom, virility, virginity or permissiveness.

HALO Symbol of divinity or sanctity, originally based on the nimbus that surrounds the sun. Used particularly in Christian art, the halo is thought to have been first used on pagan sun gods, such as Mithras. Halos also appear in Buddhist spiritual traditions.

HAMMER As a weapon the hammer is a symbol of male strength, linked with the power of the sun and the gods of war. As a tool the hammer can appear as a symbol of protection or of divine skill.

HAMMER AND SICKLE Symbol of communism's unification of the working classes, combing the sickle as a symbol of agricultural workers, and the hammer, symbol of industrial workers.

  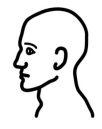   

HAND Symbol of temporal and spiritual power, action, strength and protection.

HAND OF FATIMA A symbol of the hand of God and of the five fundamentals of Islam: faith, prayer, pilgrimage, fasting and charity. Used extensively in Islamic countries as a protective and good luck charm.

HAPPINESS Rune.

HARE A lunar animal linked with divinity, menstruation and fertility. Because of its links with divinity it has sometimes been a forbidden food.

HARP Widespread use in ritual and sacred ceremony; in the Old Testament associated with Jewish nationhood. The magical harp of the Dagda (Celtic) could play music suitable for every occasion and had the power to send its enemies to sleep. The three-stringed harp used in ancient Egypt symbolized the three seasons of flood, growth and dryness.

HAWK Solar emblem of victory, superiority, aspiration, spirit, light and liberty.

HAZEL Symbol of divinity, wisdom, fertility and rain. A hazel wand was the instrument of northern European magicians and wizards.

HEAD In some traditions the location of the soul, associated with fertility and phallic symbolism, instrument of reason and thought.

HEART An ancient symbol whose original meaning is not known. Graphically related to fire. Signifies love; also appears with religious meaning among the Aztecs, Hindus, Buddhists, Muslims, Jews, Celts and Taoists.

HEART ON FIRE/FLAMING HEART Symbol of an ardent Christian, but also, in art, an attribute of charity and profane passion.

HEARTH/FIREPLACE Symbol of the home, of comfort, security and human community. For the Romans, it was the site of the household guardian spirits (lares), for the Aztecs the sacred place of Ometecuhtli, who was believed to live at the heart of the universe and in the heart of all people.

HEDGEHOG A symbol of wealth in China and Japan; in medieval Europe associated with greed and gluttony. In parts of Central Asia and Africa it is associated with the sun (because of the ray pattern made by its spines) and the invention of fire.

HELMET Symbol of protection, but also linked with invisible power.

HERMAPHRODITE Used in botany for double-sexed plants.

HEMESH HAND A Jewish variation of the hand of Fatima with similar protective symbolism.

HEPTAGRAM This star contains all the symbolism of the number 7.

HERALDIC DAGGER Used in printed text as a sign for note.

HERMES Sign of the god.

HERMES Sign of the god, variation.

HERMES Sign of the god, variation.

HERON Emblem of the morning sun.

HEXAGON Geometric shape, important in Islam as a directional.

 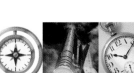

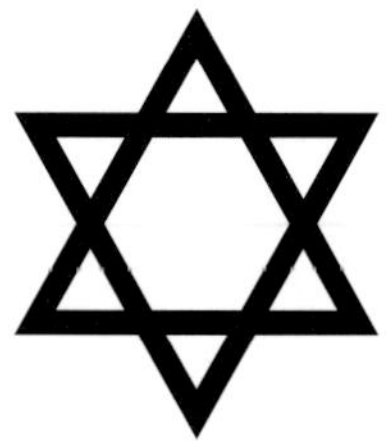

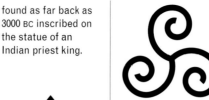

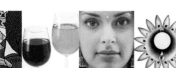

Hexagram Based on the triangle, an ancient sign for the Jewish kingdom.

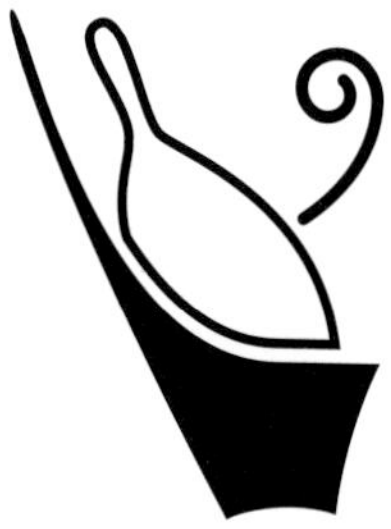

Hieroglyph Symbolizing the unification of Egypt.

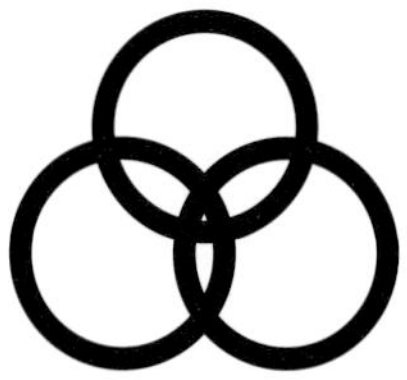

High Spiritual dignity.

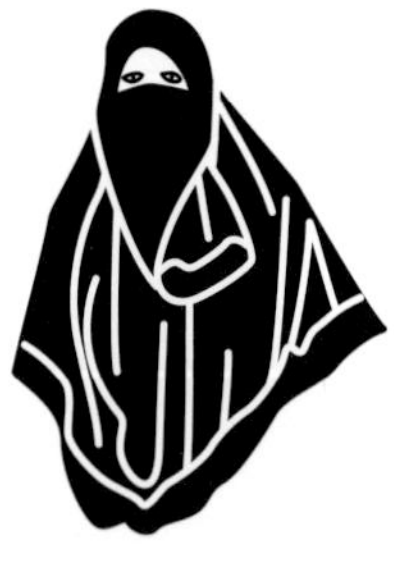

Hijab An Islamic item of clothing that carries various symbolic interpretations, including liberation and oppression. For many of those who wear it, it is an expression of their love for God.

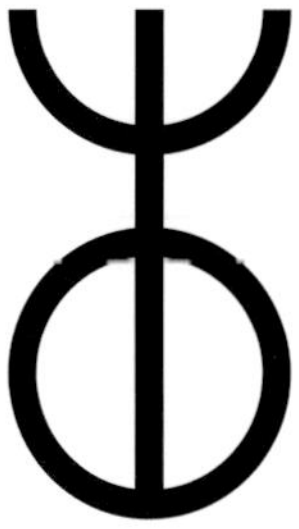

Hindu/hinduism

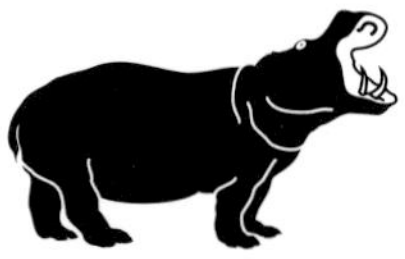

Hippopotamus In ancient Egypt, a female hippo was a fertility symbol and worshipped as an upright hippopotamus goddess. In the Old Testament, the hippo is a symbol of brute force.

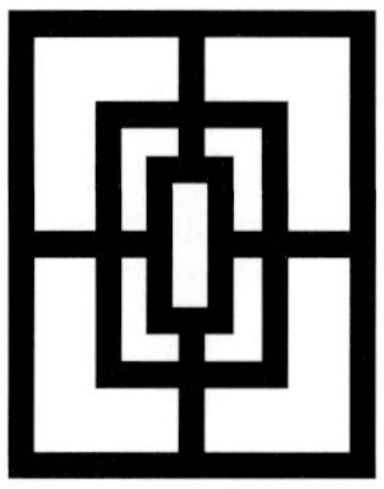

Hnefatafl A design for a games board used by the Vikings.

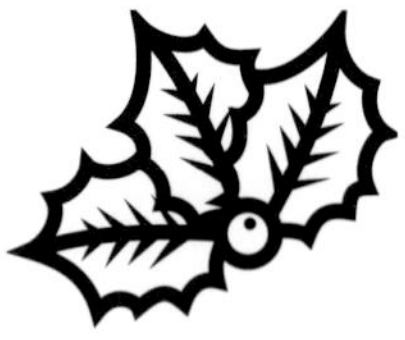

Holly A symbol of hope and joy.

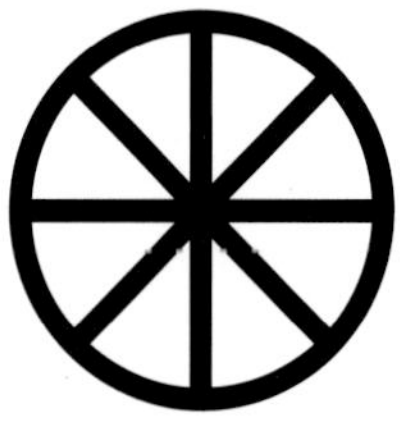

Holy sign From India around 4,000 years ago. Also found on Japanese Buddha statues from the 8th century.

Holy spirit According to some sources this Christian sign is derived from a stylized dove. This sign was also used in alchemy to signify the spirit of a substance.

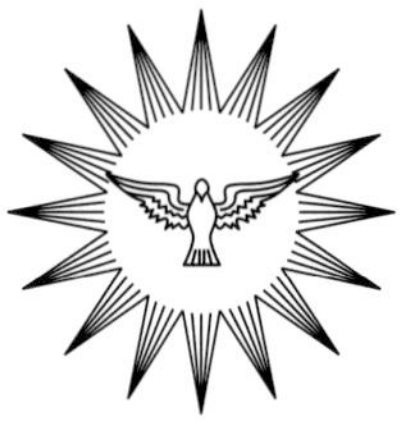

Holy spirit An early Christian symbol, one of those found inscribed in the catacombs of Roman Palestine in the years of Christian persecution.

Holy trinity This shape, denoting the unity of three, is used extensively in the architecture of churches and cathedrals. The sign itself, however, is ancient, and has been found as far back as 3000 BC inscribed on the statue of an Indian priest king.

Holy trinity A triquetras variation.

Holy trinity Another triquetras variation.

Holy trinity Variation.

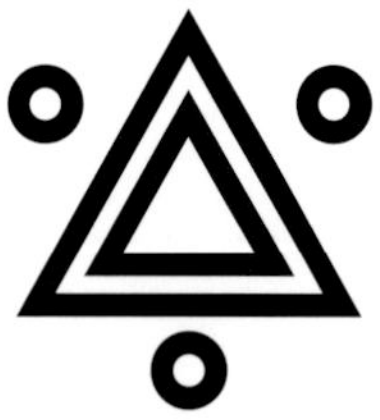

Holy trinity A Spanish variation.

Homecomings A sign from the Hopi Indians of Arizona, also symbolizes several returns or tribal migration.

Homosexual See Male

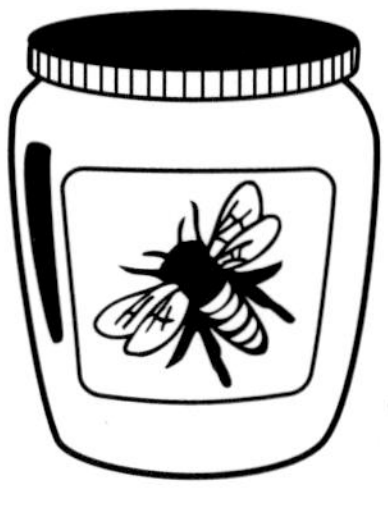

Honey Linked with the gods, purity, inspiration, eloquence and plenty.

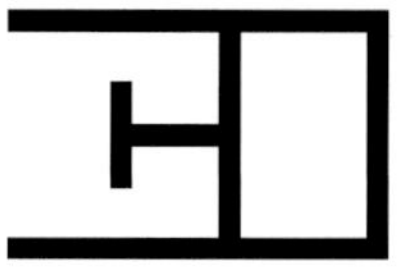

Honey Alchemistic sign.

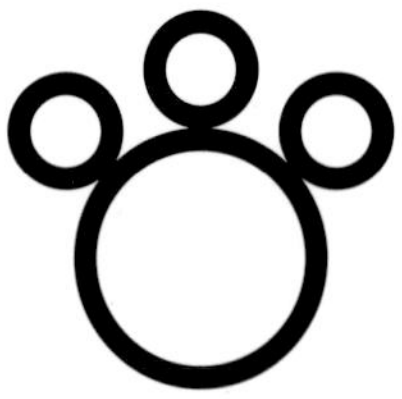

Honey Alchemistic, variation.

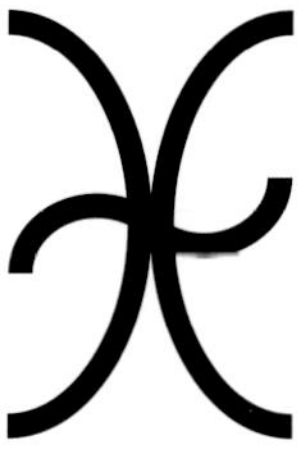

Honey Alchemistic, variation.

Hood Associated with magic and the power to make its wearer invisible. Freudian phallic symbol.

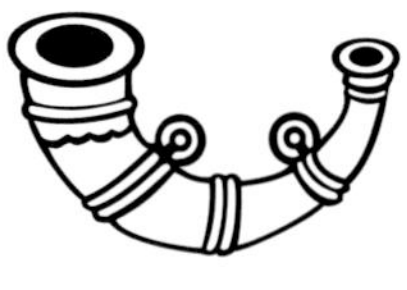

Horn Symbol of power and strength associated with the animals that have them. A bull's horn is a female lunar symbol (the crescent moon is horn-shaped), and associated with fertility; a ram's horn is a male, solar symbol, associated with virility.

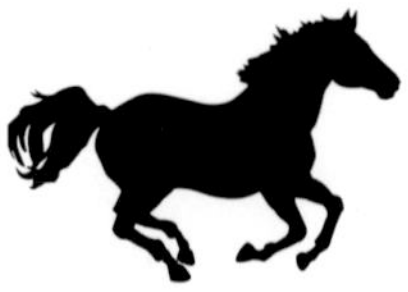

Horse Symbol of animal vitality, velocity and beauty, also associated with the power of wind, storm, fire, waves and running water.

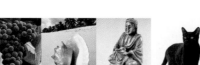

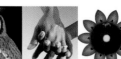

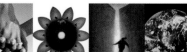

HORSESHOE Ancient protective symbol, with heel uppermost it is used in magic to call on the protection of the moon.

HORUS Ancient Egyptian solar god, symbol of cosmic wholeness.

HOUR Time sign, alchemistic.

HOUR Time sign, alchemistic, representation of hourglass.

HOURGLASS Symbol of time, and its inevitable passing.

HWEMUDUA Measuring stick, Ghanaian adinkra sign, meaning the need to strive for the best quality, whether in production of goods or in human endeavours.

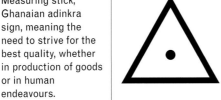

HYDRA The many-headed dragon serpent of Greek myth symbolizes the difficulty in conquering our vices.

HYE WON HYE Ghanaian adinkra sign meaning "that which cannot be burnt". This symbol gets its meaning from traditional priests that were able to walk on fire without burning their feet, an inspiration to others to endure and overcome difficulties.

IBIS A sacred symbol of wisdom for the ancient Egyptians.

ICE GRANULES Hail, meteorology

IGLOO Inuit symbol of their culture and way of life.

INFINITE Modern mathematical sign for infinitely great sum or number or indefinite number.

INFINITY Referring to time, distance or numbers.

ING Rune for Ng.

INGZ Rune, associated with fertility.

IRON Alchemistic sign.

IRON Alchemistic sign, variation.

IS Rune for I.

ISHTAR Goddess, queen of the heavens for the Babylonians and Assyrians, also god of childbirth.

ISLAM Made up of the morning star and the morning moon.

ISLAND A symbol of non-celestial heaven, a magical other place set apart from the real world.

ISOMORPH/ CONGRUENT In mathematical and geometrical systems.

IVY Symbol of immortality and also friendship; in the classical world also associated with vegetative abundance and sensuality, hence Dionysus/Bacchus (god of wine) is often depicted wearing an ivy crown.

JACKAL Symbol of destructiveness or evil in India, but in ancient Egypt worshipped as Anubis, god of embalming.

JAGUAR Linked with divination, royalty, magic, the spirit world, the earth, the moon and fertility. An important icon in shamanic traditions.

JARA Rune for J.

JESUS CHRIST

JEUNE BRETAGNE
The Celtic separatist movement in Brittany, France. The symbol was originally a Celtic one associated with migration.

JEWELS Symbols of purity, refinement and superiority. In Eastern traditions they embody spiritual knowledge.

JUICE/SAP
Alchemistic sign.

JUNO Asteroid.

JUNO Asteroid, archaic variation.

JUNO Asteroid, variation.

JUPITER The planet.

KANGAROO A symbol of modern-day Australia, traditionally associated with powerful mothering instincts (it carries its young in its pouch and is a fierce fighter) and with ancestor spirits.

KAUN Rune meaning boil or pustule.

KEN Rune for K.

KEY Through its power to lock and unlock doors, the key is a symbol of spiritual and secular authority, of access to sacred and temporal wealth. In Christianity for example, Christ gave St Peter the keys to heaven and earth, while in West Africa, a bunch of gold keys on a ring are part of court regalia, symbolizing the wealth of the state. In Japan, the key is a symbol of happiness because of its power to unlock the rice pantry.

KINTINKANTAN
Ghanain adinkra sign for puffed-up extravagance.

KITE Used as an oracular device in China and Japan; the Japanese flew kites for good health and to secure a good harvest. Chinese kites decorated with butterflies symbolized prayers for the souls of the dead and the living.

KNOT In art, literature and sacred tradition, knots symbolize the power to bind and to set free; in ancient Egypt the knot of Isis (a type of Ankh with arms folded down) was the emblem of life and immortality. Knots can be used to symbolize love and marriage, A recurring motif in Celtic art, its symbolism linked to the ouroboros, the perpetual moving and joining together of human and cosmic activities. A loose interwoven knot symbolizes infinity or longevity. Tight knots symbolize union, but also blockage or protection.

KU KLUX KLAN The symbol of the racist organization of USA.

LABYRINTH See Maze

LADDER One of the symbolic links to mountains, also a symbol of ascension, aspiration and success.

LADDER OF TRANSMIGRATION
Medieval Christian sign for the soul's pilgrimage from earthly existence to paradise.

LAGU Rune for L, meaning water or sea.

LAMB One of the earliest symbols for Christ, emblem of purity, sacrifice, renewal, redemption, innocence and gentleness. Important sacrificial and redemptive symbol for Islam and Judaism.

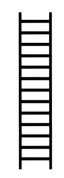

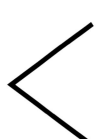

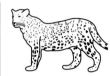

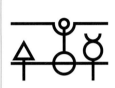

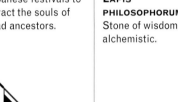

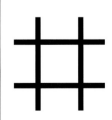

LAMP/LANTERN Symbol of spirit, truth and life. In shrines or on altars symbol of devotion and the presence of divinity. In art personification of vigilance. A Chinese lantern is a fertility symbol, used in Chinese and Japanese festivals to attract the souls of dead ancestors.

LANCE Associated with Christ's Passion, also with chivalry, symbol of masculine, phallic, earthly power. A broken lance symbolizes the experienced soldier

LAND OF EGYPT Associated with symbol for return or homecoming.

LANTERN See Lamp

LAPIS LAZULI Alchemistic sign.

LAPIS PHILOSOPHORUM Stone of wisdom, alchemistic.

LAUREL The leaves of the laurel or bay tree were, for the Greco-Roman world, symbols of victory, peace, purification, divination and immortality. Laurel also had talismanic significance in North Africa, and in China it is the tree under which the lunar hare produces the elixir of immortality.

LAUREL LEAF WREATH Linked to Apollo, Greco-Roman victory crown for both warriors and poets.

LEAD Alchemistic sign.

LEAD Alchemistic, variation.

LEAD Early chemistry.

LEAD Old chemists sign.

LEAD Alchemistic, variation also musical notation meaning to raise a half tone. In old pharmacology it was used to mean

"take in God's name". In modern use it is called the hash sign and is used on telephones.

LEAD SULPHATE Alchemistic sign.

LEMON Symbol of bitterness, failure or disappointment, in Christian art can represent faithfulness.

LEO Zodiac sign.

LEO Zodiac sign, variation.

LEOPARD Often associated with wildness, aggression and battle; in antiquity, a symbol of strength and fertility and an attribute of Dionysus; a symbol of the supreme judicial authority of the Kings of Benin (West Africa).

LESBIANISM See Love between women

LIBRA Zodiac sign.

LIGHTHOUSE Symbol of safety and protection in the face of danger; in Early Christian art, associated with Christ, also the heavenly harbour into which the soul sails after the dangerous journey through life. Freudian phallic symbol.

LIGHTNING Modern western sign for lightening made from the two signs for danger, heat together with the arrow sign for directed movement.

LIGHTNING Variation, linked with Fascism, also rune for 's'.

LILY Identified with Christian piety, purity and innocence. In older traditions associated with fertility and erotic love and the fertility of the Earth Goddess. Symbol of fecundity in ancient Greece and Egypt.

LIME Alchemistic.

LIME Early chemistry.

LINE Straight, diagonal, in modern iconography signifies forbidden or cancelled when over another sign.

LINE Straight, horizontal, represents the base, the earth, or land. Can also mean to link, increase or decrease when placed over or under another sign.

LINE Straight, vertical, one of the basic elements in western ideography. Stands for unity,

oneness, the self, authority, power. Also symbol for yang, the active, powerful, warm, extrovert and masculine dimensions of the universe.

LINES Three identical parallel and vertical, signifies three units, also active intellect.

LINES Three identical, parallel and horizontal, similarity in one dimension, used in meteorology to indicate mist.

LINES Two identical, parallel and horizontal, equals, a doubling of the uniting and linking quality of a single horizontal line.

LINES Two identical, parallel and vertical, symbol for yin, the passive, receptive, material dimension of the universe.

LINGA A sculpted upright phallus common throughout India. A cult image and sacred symbol of the male, creative principle (Hindu), associated with Shiva, the divine power of creation, and the "world axis". The feminine counterpart of the linga is the yoni.

LION Solar animal invested with divine qualities; symbol of royal power and dominion, military victory, bravery, vigilance and fortitude. Royal emblem of England and Scotland and of British imperial power in the 19th century. In China and Japan the lion is protective.

LIZARD Symbol of evil (Greco-Roman, Christianity, Maori). Among Native American tribes, associated with shamanic powers and vision quests as well as strength (the Plains Dakota). For Aboriginal Australians the

frill-necked lizard (kendi) is a powerful rainmaker. A symbol of a peaceful household for the Babanki (Cameroon).

LOGR Rune for onion or water, stream or sea.

LOOSEN/UNSCREW Modern.

LOTUS FLOWER Ancient and prolific symbol in Egypt, India, China and Japan. Symbol of birth, cosmic life, the divine, human spiritual growth and the soul's potential to achieve perfection.

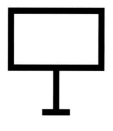

LOTUS FLOWER An ancient Egyptian mystical symbol used to signify the Earth.

LOVE BETWEEN WOMEN Lesbianism, modern ideogram.

LOZENGE The rhombus or diamond shape – one of Chinese Eight Treasures, representing good fortune.

LUTE In China symbol of the scholar and of harmony in marriage and government. In Renaissance art popular emblem of the lover; if shown with strings broken can be a symbol of discord.

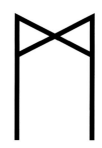

LYE Alchemistic sign.

LYRE Symbol of divine harmony, musical inspiration and divination. Linked with Orpheus. In myth it was invented by Hermes, who gave it to Apollo, whose attribute it became.

MADR Rune for M, meaning, man or human. Also known as mann.

MAGNESIUM Early chemistry.

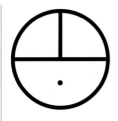

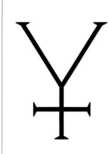

MALE HOMOSEXUAL LOVE Modern.

MAN/THE MALE There is no one symbol that represents the male principle, but this is a symbolic theme that underlies most of the world's cultures: the principle of the patriarch. Less potent today, it is still important, and carries associations such as the sun, law, authority and the warlike spirit.

MANDRAKE Believed in the Middle Ages to have magical powers; a symbol for sorcery and witchcraft.

MAP OF THE WORLD Ideogram from the Middle Ages, the vertical line signified the Mediterranean sea, the horizontal line to the left was the Nile, that to the right the Don River, the upper right section was Europe, the left Africa, the bottom Asia. The full point in Asia was Jerusalem.

MARCASITE/FOOL'S GOLD Also iron sulphate, alchemistic.

MARS The planet, named after the Roman god of war, in Greece known as Ares. Became the sign for iron (the metal used for weapons) due to Mars' link with war.

MARS The planet, variation, also sign for iron.

MASK Dramatic means of projecting symbolism in religion, ritual and theatre. Symbol of concealment or illusion, in Western art an attribute of deceit personified, of vice and of night.

MAYPOLE European folkloric phallic symbol, spring emblem of fertility and solar renewal, linked to classical spring rites.

MAZE/LABYRINTH Possibly linking back to the cave systems in which humanity once lived; ambivalent symbolism includes protection, initiation, death or rebirth, choices and life direction.

MELTING OVEN/FORGE Alchemistic.

MENORAH The nine-candelabra of Judaism, symbol of the nation of Israel.

MERCURY Alchemistic.

MERCURY Alchemistic, variation.

MERCURY Alchemistic, variation.

MERCURY Sign of the planet.

MERCURY Sign of the planet, variation; also for mercury, metal, also poison in early chemistry.

MERCURY Sign of the planet, ancient Greek variation.

MERCURY Sign of the planet, variation.

MERCURY Sign of the planet, variation.

MERMAID See Siren

METAL Alchemistic.

MIGRATION A Hopi Indian sign centred around the idea of several returns, or homecoming.

MIGRATION Variation, Celtic, more recently adopted by Jeune Bretagne, a French separatist movement.

MIHRAB Islamic, niche in the wall of a mosque indicating the direction of Mecca, decorated with geometric motifs and text from the Qur'an.

MINARET A slim tower connected to an Islamic mosque. Derived from an Arabic word meaning "to give off light", the minaret acts as a beacon of illumination to the surrounding community – it is from here that the muezzin calls the faithful to prayer.

MIRAGE

MIRROR Symbol of veracity, self-knowledge, purity, enlightenment and divination. Sometimes in Western art seen as symbol of pride, vanity or lust. Linked with magic, especially divination.

MISTLETOE Sacred to the Celtic druids as a fertility and regeneration symbol, has since been attributed with fire, lightning and rebirth. The berries were once credited with healing properties.

MITSUBISHI Corporate emblem of the Japanese firm.

MIX/MIXTURE Alchemistic.

MIX Alchemistic, variation.

MONKEY Its imitative skills make it a symbol of human vanity and other folly.

MOON Egyptian hieroglyph.

MOON/MONTH Hittite hieroglyphic system.

MOON, NEW In astrology symbolizes human receptivity, instinct, subconscious, emotional life and ability to react. Also used as a symbol for the mother, or women in general. Alchemical sign for silver.

MOON (WANING) Used, together with a star, as the symbol for the Roman province of Illyricum and then for Constantinople. Later it developed into the sign for the Islamic faith.

MOTHER AND CHILD Appears on pre-Columbian engravings and rock paintings in Arizona, and on an Etruscan vase from around 550 BC. Also found in medieval churches throughout Europe, and in ancient stone structures in Sweden.

MOUNTAIN Symbol of transcendence, eternity, purity and spiritual ascent. Associated with immortals, heroes, sanctified prophets and gods.

MOUSE Associated with female sexuality, lechery and voracity (Greco-Roman), although a white mouse is a good luck symbol (Roman). Also associated with destructive, dark forces, stealth and cunning (Celtic) in European folklore during the Middle Ages; mice were associated with witches and the souls of the dead; infestations of mice were considered a divine punishment.

MOUTH An open mouth associated with the power of the spirit to speak, the inspiration of the soul; alternatively it can symbolize destructive forces, things being "eaten" and "devoured".

MUSHROOM Symbol of life arising from death, longevity and happiness in China; souls of the reborn in some parts of central Europe and Africa. Folklore links it with the supernatural.

MUSICAL NOTE In the Middle Ages, also (reversed) used as ideogram by the Sumerians around 3000 BC.

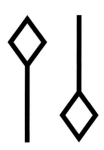

NANNAN Very ancient sign for moon god later known as Sin in the Euphrates-Tigris region. For the Babylonians the sign was linked with Venus and the sun.

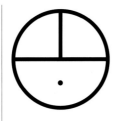

MALE HOMOSEXUAL LOVE Modern.

MAN/THE MALE There is no one symbol that represents the male principle, but this is a symbolic theme that underlies most of the world's cultures: the principle of the patriarch. Less potent today, it is still important, and carries associations such as the sun, law, authority and the warlike spirit.

MANDRAKE Believed in the Middle Ages to have magical powers; a symbol for sorcery and witchcraft.

MAP OF THE WORLD Ideogram from the Middle Ages, the vertical line signified the Mediterranean sea, the horizontal line to the left was the Nile, that to the right the Don River, the upper right section was Europe, the left Africa, the bottom Asia. The full point in Asia was Jerusalem.

MARCASITE/FOOL'S GOLD Also iron sulphate, alchemistic.

MARS The planet, named after the Roman god of war, in Greece known as Ares. Became the sign for iron (the metal used for weapons) due to Mars' link with war.

MARS The planet, variation, also sign for iron.

MASK Dramatic means of projecting symbolism in religion, ritual and theatre. Symbol of concealment or illusion, in Western art an attribute of deceit personified, of vice and of night.

MAYPOLE European folkloric phallic symbol, spring emblem of fertility and solar renewal, linked to classical spring rites.

MAZE/LABYRINTH Possibly linking back to the cave systems in which humanity once lived; ambivalent symbolism includes protection, initiation, death or rebirth, choices and life direction.

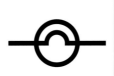

MELTING OVEN/ FORGE Alchemistic.

MENORAH The nine-candelabra of Judaism, symbol of the nation of Israel.

MERCURY Alchemistic.

MERCURY Alchemistic, variation.

MERCURY Alchemistic, variation.

MERCURY Sign of the planet.

MERCURY Sign of the planet, variation; also for mercury, metal, also poison in early chemistry.

MERCURY Sign of the planet, ancient Greek variation.

MERCURY Sign of the planet, variation.

MERCURY Sign of the planet, variation.

MERMAID See Siren

METAL Alchemistic.

110

MIGRATION A Hopi Indian sign centred around the idea of several returns, or homecoming.

MIGRATION Variation, Celtic, more recently adopted by Jeune Bretagne, a French separatist movement.

MIHRAB Islamic, niche in the wall of a mosque indicating the direction of Mecca, decorated with geometric motifs and text from the Qur'an.

MINARET A slim tower connected to an Islamic mosque. Derived from an Arabic word meaning "to give off light", the minaret acts as a beacon of illumination to the surrounding community – it is from here that the muezzin calls the faithful to prayer.

MIRAGE

MIRROR Symbol of veracity, self-knowledge, purity, enlightenment and divination. Sometimes in Western art seen as symbol of pride, vanity or lust. Linked with magic, especially divination.

MISTLETOE Sacred to the Celtic druids as a fertility and regeneration symbol, has since been attributed with fire, lightning and rebirth. The berries were once credited with healing properties.

MITSUBISHI Corporate emblem of the Japanese firm.

MIX/MIXTURE Alchemistic.

MIX Alchemistic, variation.

MONKEY Its imitative skills make it a symbol of human vanity and other folly.

MOON Egyptian hieroglyph.

MOON/MONTH Hittite hieroglyphic system.

MOON, NEW In astrology symbolizes human receptivity, instinct, subconscious, emotional life and ability to react. Also used as a symbol for the mother, or women in general. Alchemical sign for silver.

MOON (WANING) Used, together with a star, as the symbol for the Roman province of Illyricum and then for Constantinople. Later it developed into the sign for the Islamic faith.

MOTHER AND CHILD Appears on pre-Columbian engravings and rock paintings in Arizona, and on an Etruscan vase from around 550 BC. Also found in medieval churches throughout Europe, and in ancient stone structures in Sweden.

MOUNTAIN Symbol of transcendence, eternity, purity and spiritual ascent. Associated with immortals, heroes, sanctified prophets and gods.

MOUSE Associated with female sexuality, lechery and voracity (Greco-Roman), although a white mouse is a good luck symbol (Roman). Also associated with destructive, dark forces, stealth and cunning (Celtic) in European folklore during the Middle Ages; mice were associated with witches and the souls of the dead; infestations of mice were considered a divine punishment.

MOUTH An open mouth associated with the power of the spirit to speak, the inspiration of the soul; alternatively it can symbolize destructive forces, things being "eaten" and "devoured".

MUSHROOM Symbol of life arising from death, longevity and happiness in China; souls of the reborn in some parts of central Europe and Africa. Folklore links it with the supernatural.

MUSICAL NOTE In the Middle Ages, also (reversed) used as ideogram by the Sumerians around 3000 BC.

NANNAN Very ancient sign for moon god later known as Sin in the Euphrates-Tigris region. For the Babylonians the sign was linked with Venus and the sun.

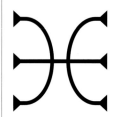

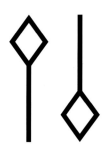
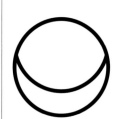

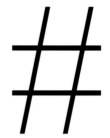
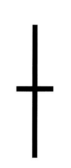

NAUDH Rune for N meaning need, misery.

NAVEL The centre of creative and psychic energy, the source of life, linked to fertility.

NAZI SS Logo of the Nazi special police unit known as the Schutz Staffeln, or SS.

NEPTUNE Sign for the planet, rare variation.

NET Symbol of catching and gathering; in the East, deities sometimes shown with a net that they use to draw people closer to them; in Christianity, it is associated with the apostles as "fishers of men". In Jungian psychology, fishing with a net can signify connecting with the unconscious.

NICKEL Calcinated copper, alchemistic.

NIED Rune for N.

NIGHT Time sign, alchemistic.

NIKE Corporate logo.

NINE As the triple triad, nine is a supremely powerful number, the most auspicious Chinese number, the most potent yang number. In mysticism it represents the triple synthesis of mind, body and spirit. Hebrew symbol of truth, Christian symbol of order within order.

NKONSONKONSON Chain links, Ghanaian adinkra symbol meaning strength within unity, used as a reminder to contribute to the community.

NOOSE A masonic symbol of the cord that binds one to life and in initiation rituals, of being born into a new life. As hangman's noose, a symbol of death and the end of life.

NOSE Associated with intuitive discernment, hence expressions such as "sniffing out the truth". In Maori culture, rubbing noses is not only a way of kissing, but symbolizes the gods breathing life into humans and is a sign of peace. In Japan, people point to their nose rather than their heart to indicate themselves.

NSORAN Sorrow or lament, Ghanaian adinkra symbol.

NSOROMMA Child of the heavens, Ghanaian adinkra symbol used as a reminder that God is father and watches over all people.

NUMBER In modern Western systems. In musical notation it is called a sharp and is an instruction to raise a half tone. Also used in early chemistry to denote air.

NUMBER 10 From the medieval clog almanacs to calculate the moon's phases.

NUT Highly symbolic in the Jewish tradition, the nut is the symbol of the scholar, and represents virtue in that the beginning and end, seed and fruit are one and the same. The Romans considered the nut a fertility symbol in both humans and animals.

NYAME BIRIBI WO SORO God is in the heavens. Ghanaian adinkra symbol.

NYAME NNWU NA MAWU God never dies, therefore I cannot die. Ghanaian adinkra symbol reminding people of immortality.

OAK Linked with nobility and endurance, sacred to thunder gods of the Celts, Greeks and Germanic tribes, symbol of male potency and wisdom but linked to mother goddesses and the Dryads, oak nymphs.

OBELISK Rectangular, tapering pillar, Egyptian symbol of the sun god, Ra, topped by a reflective pyramid that caught the light.

OCTAGON Draws on the symbolism of the number eight, emblem of renewal, and combining the symbolism of the square and the circle.

OCTAGRAM OF CREATION Gnostic, also Nordic invocation of magic and protection.

OIL Alchemistic.

OLYMPIC GAMES Five linked rings symbolizing the five continents of the world that participate in the sporting event.

OM SYMBOL (Aum), the greeting of peace in India. The symbol represents the four states of consciousness: awake, dreaming, sleeping, without dreams and the transcendental state.

OMEGA The last letter of the Greek alphabet.

ONE A symbol of God, emblem of primordial unity, could also stand for the sun or light, and the origin of life. Confucian perfect entity. Symbol of beginning, the self and loneliness.

ONE Roman numeral, singular, individual, emperor, Jesus. Used in English speaking world to signify the first person.

OPEL For their corporate logo this car manufacturer used the ancient sign for victory.

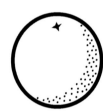

ORANGE Commonly a symbol of fertility.

ORB See Globe

OSTRICH In ancient Egypt an ostrich feather was a symbol of justice and truth. The burying of its head in the sand is a modern symbol of avoiding the truth.

OTHEL Rune for O.

OTTER Often associated with lunar symbolism from its periodic nature of diving and rising in water. A Romanian folk song tells of otters guiding the souls of the dead. The otter often also symbolizes laughter, playfulness and mischievousness.

OUROBOROS A serpent in circular formation with tail in its mouth, symbol of cyclic time, eternity and the indivisible, self-sustaining character of Nature.

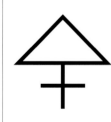

OWL Associated with magic, the otherworld, wisdom and prophecy in many traditions.

OX Universally benevolent symbol of strength, patience, submissiveness and steady toil. Christian emblem of sacrificial Christ. Sacrificial animal in the ancient world. Taoist and Buddhist symbol of the sage.

PACHUCO CROSS An identifying sign, often used as a tattoo, by Hispanic-American street gangs.

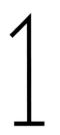

PAGODA Sacred building in the Buddhist tradition, the diminishing tiers symbolize spiritual ascent.

PALLAS Sign of the asteroid.

PANTHER The panther commonly depicts desire and power. However, in ancient Christian symbolism the panther was one of three animals representing chastity. The black panther is a feminine symbol of the night, death and rebirth.

PARASOL/UMBRELLA Symbol for the dome of Heaven in ancient China. The parasol was Vishnu's symbol and also an emblem of the Buddha himself. The parasol is often also a solar symbol suggesting the rank, authority and even the halo of the king who is shaded by it. In an everyday sense the parasol represents protection.

PARROT A symbol of the sun and the coming of the rainy season in Native American lore. In Hinduism, Kama – god of love – rides a parrot across three worlds spreading love and desire.

PARZ A very early rune, later came to mean secret, mystery, initiation in Anglo-Saxon literature.

PAWNSHOP Originally part of the Medici family arms, who were rich money lenders.

PEACE Christian.

PEACH A very important symbol in Chinese culture with many meanings; associated with immortality, an emblem of marriage, a fertility symbol.

PEAR The pear is a mother, or love, symbol with erotic associations that are probably due to its shape. Associated with Aphrodite and Hera in classical mythology. A longevity symbol in China.

PELICAN Christian symbol of self-sacrificial love, based on the medieval misconception that the birds tore their own breasts to feed their young. This link with shedding its own blood led to its use to represent Christ.

PEN A Freudian phallic symbol, also associated with the executive function and the power of reason. In the Sufi tradition the Supreme Pen represents Universal Intelligence.

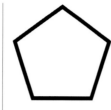

PENTAGON Associated with the planet Venus, used in a few established Western ideographic systems.

PENTAGRAM/ PENTACLE Used since 4000 BC with unknown significance, especially by the Sumerians, until Pythagorean mysticism defined it as a symbol of the human being. Known as Solomon's Seal in medieval Jewish mysticism.

PEORTH Rune for P.

PER CENT Modern.

PHALEC Used in Kabbalistic mysticism for the spirit of Mars.

PHILOSOPHER'S STONE Alchemistic.

PHOENIX The legendary bird that renews itself in fire became the most famous of all rebirth symbols, a resurrection emblem and eventually the symbol of the indomitable human spirit.

PIG Ambiguous symbolism of gluttony, selfishness, lust, obstinacy and ignorance, but also motherhood, fertility, prosperity and happiness.

PIPE In Native American culture tobacco was a sacred herb. Smoking shared pipes was a social activity based around religious ceremony or tribal alliances.

PISCES Zodiac sign.

PISCES Zodiac sign, ancient Greek variation.

PLAITED SIGN Nordic design pattern.

PLATINUM A metal discovered in the mid-1800s, its sign is a combination of those for gold and silver.

PLEIADES Magical amulet seal.

PLIMSOLL MARK Named after its inventor, printed on the sides of cargo ships to give visible checks as to the safety of the cargo's weight, depending on which waters the ship was sailing in.

PLOUGH Symbol of peace, also a male fertility symbol, the male plough entering the female earth. Also a thematic symbol of man's farming activity, pushing back the wilderness and taming it to produce food. Counter-balance to the sword, as an anti-war concept.

PLUTO Sign of the planet, the most common variation.

PLUTO Sign of the planet, variation.

PLUTO Sign of the planet, variation.

POLARIS Fixed star, magical amulet seal, Kabbalism.

POMEGRANATE Strongly identified with sexual temptation, also with unity, linked to fertility, love and marriage.

POSEIDON Sign of the god.

POTASH Alchemistic.

POTASSIUM CARBONATE Late alchemy and early chemistry.

POUND STERLING British currency.

PRAYER BEADS Used in religious contexts, such as Catholicism and Buddhism, as an aid to remembering specific prayers or sequences of prayers. The number of beads in the string usually has symbolic meaning.

PRAYER STICK An aid to prayer in shamanic traditions, and a link with God.

PRAYER WHEEL Tibetan, an aid to prayer for Buddhists and Hindus that is spun round as the prayer unfolds. Its turning movement therefore is a symbol in itself of the cycles of birth, death and rebirth.

PRECIPITATION Alchemistic.

PROCYON Astrological sign for the star procyon.

PROTECTION An example of several similar structures that were drawn on barns and houses for protection or good fortune.

PUMPKIN In China, and in feng shui the pumpkin symbolizes prosperity and abundance. A pumpkin with a face carved out of it is known as a Jack O' Lantern, which is a symbol of Halloween.

PURIFICATION Alchemistic.

PYRAMID Carrying the same symbolism as the triangle, one of the most powerful and versatile geometric symbols.

QUAIL Chinese symbol of light, also warmth, ardour and courage. In Greek and Hindu traditions the quail is a symbol of renewal of life and return of the sun.

QUESTION MARK Modern, denoting a question in written text.

QUINCUNX Astrology, the inconjunct aspect: a 150-degree angle between planets as seen from Earth.

QUINTESSENCE Alchemistic.

QUINTILE Astrology.

RABBIT Strong moon association and therefore linked with menstruation and fertility in most traditions. Folkloric symbol of harmless guile.

RAD Rune for R.

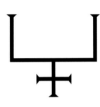

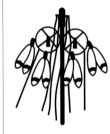

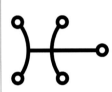

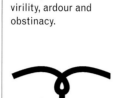

RADIATION Used since antiquity for radiation of light, in modern usage release of energy or radiation, in comic strips fistfights and explosions.

RAIDO Rune associated with raiding, journey.

RAIN Vital symbol of fecundity linked to divine blessings or punishments. Emblem of purity.

RAM Symbol of solar energy, as first sign of the zodiac represents renewal of fertility and return of spring. Also symbolizes virility, ardour and obstinacy.

RAPHAEL Symbol of the archangel.

RAT Symbol of fecundity, also destructiveness and avarice. Generally negative associations but in folkloric traditions it is a symbol of knowingness, and in Asian traditions it is associated with gods of wisdom, success or prosperity.

RATTLE Used in shamanic rituals, and a symbol of the shaman him/herself and their position as a mediator between Earth and the otherworld.

RAVEN A symbol of loss, death and war in western Europe, but venerated elsewhere as a solar and oracular symbol; the messenger bird of the god Apollo in the Greek world and linked with the Roman cult of Mithras. In Africa the raven is a guide, and to Native Americans a culture hero. The Inuits have a creator god called the Raven Father, and they believed that killing a raven would bring bad weather.

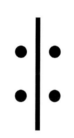

RECYCLING A modern sign for the recycling of household or industrial waste.

REEDS Japanese and Celtic symbol of purification. Fertility symbol in Mesoamerica. In classical tradition it is an emblem of Pan (he made his pipes from reeds), and in Christian symbolism it is linked to Christ's Passion from the vinegar-soaked sponge that was offered to him on the end of a reed. In Western folklore tradition, reeds were believed to protect from witchcraft.

REGULUS Star, medieval magical amulet seal.

REINDEER In cultures of the far north reindeer have lunar significance as funerary symbols, and are said to be conductors of dead souls. The flight of reindeer associated with Christmas probably originates in the flight of the Lapp shaman.

REPETITION Musical notation.

REVERSED FOUR Ancient and widespread structure found in prehistoric caves in Western Europe, meaning unknown.

RHINOCEROS An astrological symbol of the ancient Indus Calendar (3100 BC), the rhinoceros is one of four animals that surround Brahma, the Hindu god of creation.

RIBBON The symbolism of the ribbon depends more upon colour or context. Ribbons are often worn to indicate the wearer identifies with a particular cause or memory.

RICE Central emblem of growth, rebirth and fertility. Staple food in India and China and therefore has particular significance in these cultures, with links to divine nourishment. In Asia rice is used as a fecundity symbol at Indian weddings and appears in mythology as the gift of the gods to the first humans. In China rice wine was a sacred drink, and grains of rice were placed in the mouths of the dead. The Japanese god, Inari is the god of prosperity and of rice.

RING Circular symbol of eternity and therefore a prime binding symbol, also symbol of completion, continuity, strength and protection. Used as an emblem of authority, occult protective power, and as the sign of a personal pledge.

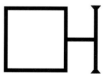

ROCK The rock commonly symbolizes that which is unchanging, enduring and motionless. In Chinese Taoist thought, rocks, as seen in landscape paintings, are associated with the qualities of the active principle, yang. Similarly in Hindu tradition rocks are embued with this same active principle. Sisyphus' rock is a symbol of the earthly desires of humans.

ROCK SALT Alchemistic.

Rod/wand, ancient symbol of supernatural power associated with the tree, the phallus and the snake.

Rose Mystic symbol of the heart; centre of the cosmic wheel; of sacred, romantic and sensual love, and of perfection.

Rosette The eight-leaf rosette is an ancient and global symbol representing birth, death and rebirth, specifically in relation to the sun or the planet Venus. In modern times rosettes made from ribbons are used to mark a victory.

Rubber Alchemistic.

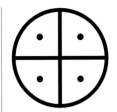

Saffron Alchemistic.

Sagittarius Zodiac sign.

Salmon Symbol of virility, fecundity, courage, wisdom and foresight. To the Celts the salmon was linked to transformation and virility. To the people of northern Europe the salmon's migration upriver made it a totem of nature's bounty and wisdom.

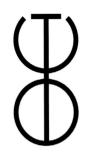

Salt Alchemistic sign.

Salt water Alchemistic sign.

Sandal Removal of sandals represents the connection between the human and the Earth: this is seen in the Masonic ritual of removing sandals, and in Moses making contact with holy ground on Mount Sinai. To the ancient Taoists winged sandals enabled the immortals to move through the air, symbolism seen also in the winged sandals of Hermes and Perseus.

Sanfoka Ghanaian adinkra symbol meaning "return and get it", signifying the importance of learning from the past.

Sap See Juice

Saturn Sign for the god.

Saturn Sign for the god, variation.

Saturn Sign for the planet.

Sauvastika Reversed swastika, Greek variation from around 500 BC.

Sauvastika Reversed swastika, associated with misfortune and bad luck.

Scales Common representation of justice, truth, balance and prudence; the weighing up of decisions and actions. In ancient Egyptian mythology, scales were used to weigh the souls of the dead, and in Christian iconography angels are often depicted with scales as the symbol of divine judgement.

Scallop shell Associated with Aphrodite, and therefore with love.

Scarab beetle Ancient Egyptian solar symbol.

Sceptre/staff Originally a male fertility symbol, implies royal or divine power and has been used as a symbol of imperial or kingly position, especially in Western art.

Scissors Ceremonial tool whose action of cutting marks the culmination and opening of a new project, as in the opening of a building. Scissors were associated with Atropos, the Fate who cut the thread of life.

Scorpio Zodiac sign.

Scorpio Zodiac sign, variation.

SCORPIO Zodiac sign, variation.

SCROLL Symbol of learning and law.

SCYTHE Farm implement used for cutting crops, associated with Roman god Saturn. In medieval iconography, an attribute of the Grim Reaper (Death).

SEA HORSE Can symbolize the male role in the birthing process, as the male animal carries its young within its own body.

SEAL OF LOA-TZU Taoist sage.

SEAL OF SOLOMON Also known as the pentagram, and the Star of David.

SEED OF THE UNIVERSE This is the Tibetan sign for the origins of the universe, also found in the coat of arms of the Aztec god Quetzalcoatl.

SERPENT/SNAKE Most significant and complex animal, symbol of primeval life force and divine self-sufficiency. Often part of creation myths; Vishnu, the Hindu creator god, rests on the coils of a great snake; in

African myths the rainbow snake links the earth with the heavens; the Aztec bird-snake divinity Quetzalcoatl does the same, and in Egypt the barge that carries the dead to the underworld enters a serpent. The snake also has sexual and agricultural fertility symbolism.

SERPENT COILED AROUND EGG Sometimes referred to as the cosmic egg, Greek symbol of the world being protected by a cosmic serpent.

SESA WORUBAN Ghanaian adinkra symbol, meaning the ability to change or transform life.

SEVEN Sacred, mystical and magical number; symbol of cosmic and spiritual order; sacred to Apollo, Osiris, Mithras and the Buddha. Symbol of perfection for Islam.

SEXUAL LOVE Modern, composed of heart sign and the arrow of Eros, one of the most widely used contemporary icons.

SHAMROCK Emblem of Ireland, supposedly from the time when St Patrick, patron saint of Ireland, used the shamrock to explain the three elements of the Holy Trinity to his congregation.

SHARK Modern associations with terror and violence.

SHEAF OF WHEAT Fertility symbol, also associated with abundance, plenty, with daily bread and with harvest time.

SHEEP Meekness and a helpless need for leadership and protection.

SHEPHERD Symbol of protection and care. Jesus Christ is portrayed in the Bible as the Good Shepherd, and this image has been widely used in Western art.

SHIELD Symbol of protection and deliverance. In the medieval chivalric period, the shield was part of a knight's badge of honour and identification. In Aboriginal myth, the shield is associated with the moon.

SHOE The shoe is commonly a symbol of possession. It is an Islamic tradition to remove one's shoes when crossing the threshold of another's house, showing one claims no possession of the property. Shoes can also signify that an individual is his or her own master.

SHOFAR A symbol of the Jewish faith, a ram's horn that is blown like a trumpet on Jewish new year.

SHOU The Chinese character for long life, used in the decoration of ceramics and textiles.

SICKLE One of the tools of the Grim Reaper, associated with death, also with harvest and agriculture. One of the parts of the sign for communism.

SIEVE Commonly symbolizes the separation of good and evil. The sieve is also used as a sifting tool of divine justice or satanic judgement.

SIGEL Rune for S.

SIGRUNE Rune linked with victory.

SIKHISM Sign of the Sikh faith.

SILVER Alchemistic.

SILVER Alchemistic, variation.

SIREN/MERMAID Seen as the embodiment of the sexual side of the female, symbol of temptation, beauty and otherness.

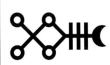

SIRIUS Star, magical amulet seal, Kabbalism.

SIX Symbol of union and equilibrium.

SKULL Potent symbol of death, used as a sign warning that a substance is poison. As part of the skull and crossbones motif is also a symbol of piratism.

SLING From the biblical story of David and Goliath, the sling has been used as a symbol of the triumph of the weak.

SMA Egyptian, union.

SMOKE An ascension symbol; means of communication on cosmic and mundane level for Native Americans. Also a symbol of concealment.

SNAIL Usually a lunar symbol associated with cyclical or periodic processes in nature. In coming out and returning to its shell the snail is indicative of an eternal homecoming. The snail is also associated with the sexual symbolism of the vulva; the Aztecs considered it to be a symbol of conception, pregnancy and birth.

SNOW Six-pointed crystal; modern sign for freezing.

SOLAR ECLIPSE Symbol of cosmic danger; in ancient cultures was a symbol of fear.

SPACE ROCKET Symbol of human endeavour and soaring ambition.

SPADES Suit of cards, associated with fighting, destiny, logical thinking, and death. Originally iconic sign for sword.

SPEAR As the lance, a symbol of masculine, phallic and earthly power. Associated with chivalry and with the Passion of Christ, from the spear that pierced his side. The broken lance is an attribute of St George, patron saint of England, and symbolizes the experienced soldier.

SPHINX In ancient Egypt, a monument of a human-headed lion, symbol of the sun. In ancient Greece, a riddle-spinning hybrid with wings, female human head and breasts, which Jung saw as a symbol of the devouring mother.

SPICA Sign of the star.

SPIDER Folkloric links with oncoming rain, also with gifts from Heaven.

SPIRAL The clockwise spiral starts from the middle, symbolizes water, power, independent movement and migration. One of the most important and ancient symbols; most common of all decorative motifs throughout cultures. As an open and flowing line it suggests extension, evolution and continuity.

SPIRAL Maori Koru, the Polynesian spiral has sexual symbolism and is based on the uncurling fern leaf. It shows the close link between spiral motifs and natural phenomena.

SPIRAL OF LIFE Found in the Bronze Age in Ireland, this sign is drawn in one single line without beginning or end.

SPLIT/CLEAVE Appears in earliest Chinese and other ancient writing systems.

SPRING Time sign, alchemistic.

SPRING Time sign, Germanic.

SQUARE An expression of the two dimensions that constitute a surface; symbol of land, field, ground, or the earth element. Thought to mean realization or materialization in Egyptian hieroglyphs.

SQUARE WITHIN A CIRCLE In Chinese symbolism this represents Earth. In Beijing the temple of Earth is constructed on this principle, whereas the temple of Heaven is a circle within a square.

SQUARE, WITH CROSS In China and Japan symbolizes field or ground, not common in Western ideography.

SQUARE, WITH DOT Village in Chinese writing; urine in alchemistic; wet ground in meteorology.

SQUARE, WITHIN A SQUARE Keep, retain, keep inside or close in. Modern sign for manhole.

STAFF See Sceptre.

STAFF OF APOLLO Also known as the Latin cross; in pre-Christian times it represented the god Apollo and appeared on ancient coins. Also used in pre-Columbian America and the Euphrates–Tigris region as a sun sign.

STAFF OF THE DEVIL

STAFF OF JUPITER/ZEUS

STAFF OF ODIN

STAFF OF POSEIDON

STAFF Egyptian.

STAFF Phoenician.

STAG Solar emblem of fertility, the antlers symbolize the tree of life, the sun's rays, longevity and rebirth. Antlers have been used as headdresses for dieties; on the Celtic antlered god Cerunnus they represented spring and fecundity.

STAIRCASE Symbol of ascent and descent; in the acquisition of knowledge of the divine when rising, or of the unconscious or the occult when descending.

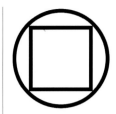
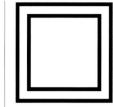

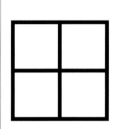
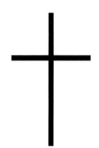

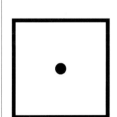

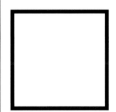

STAR Three-pointed, known as an Ethiopian emblem, a rare three-pointed star symbol.

STAR Four-pointed, also known as the sun star, denotes serious and solemn warning.

STAR Five-pointed, one of the most common and important Western ideograms; used on 35 national flags; widely used as a military and law enforcement symbol. Denotes the Bethlehem star. Used to indicate top quality.

STAR Six-pointed; rare in Western ideography but used in some United States as a policeman's badge.

STAR Eight-pointed, an ancient symbol for the goddess, or the planet, Venus, and for the Morning or Evening Star.

STAR, EASTERN Sign for the planet Venus. Common among tribal peoples in Africa and the Americas.

STAR Gnostic.

STAR OF DAVID Most well known of Jewish symbols, is supposed to be based on the shape of King David's shield, but is almost certainly more modern. Also known as the seal of Solomon, and in mystic traditions as the pentagram.

STAR OF LAKSHMI

STAR OF VENUS

STAR OF VENUS Phoenician variation.

STARFISH With its five-fold symmetry, the starfish is an esoteric symbol associated with five-pointed stars and the spiral of life.

STEEL Alchemistic.

STONES/PEBBLES Alchemistic.

STORK Symbol of longevity and filial devotion. Sacred to Greek goddess Hera. Linked to purity, piety and resurrection for Christians.

STUPA Graphical representation of a stupa symbolizing the organization of the universe: square for earth, circle for water, triangle for fire, crescent for air and droplet for ether.

SUBLIMATE Alchemistic.

SUCCESS Protection against evil, Sumerian; also Viking.

SULPHUR Alchemistic.

SULPHUR Alchemistic, variation.

SUMMER Time sign, alchemistic.

SUN Dominant symbol of creative energy in most traditions; symbol of

vitality, passion, courage and eternally renewed youth, knowledge, intellect and truth. Emblem of royalty and imperial splendour.

SUN Variation, also gold in pre-Christian Greece.

SUN Most ancient ideogram for the sun, seems to have been used in every cultural sphere on earth.

SUN Bronze Age Nordic, also prehistoric Egyptian.

SUN CROSS Danish Bronze age.

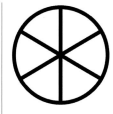

SUN CROSS Variation found in excavation of 4000 year-old Cretan city of Troy.

SUN GOD The archetypal ancient Egyptian sign, known as the Eye of Horus, and as the *wedjat*. Symbol of cosmic wholeness, and of the all-seeing power of the god Horus.

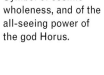

SUN/SUNLIGHT/ STARS Japanese.

SUN WHEEL Also known as the ring cross; common in the Nordic countries, pre-Columbian America, and throughout the Mediterranean about 3,500 years ago.

SUN WHEEL Used in Gaul, also sign of Taranis, Celtic god of thunder.

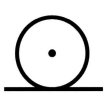

SUNRISE New day, earliest Chinese writing systems.

SWAN Romantic and ambiguous symbol of masculine light and feminine beauty in Western music and ballet. Attribute of Aphrodite and Apollo.

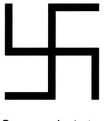

SWASTIKA Ancient ideogram first found in Sumeria about 3000 BC. Its name comes from the Sanskrit *su*, "well", and *asti* "being". Used in India, Japan and Southern Europe with various meanings, all of them positive, including as one of the symbols of the Buddha. The swastika

SWASTIKA Ancient Greek variation.

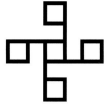

SWASTIKA Celtic variation.

SWASTIKA Christian variation.

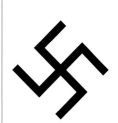

SWASTIKA Nazi variation, in which an ancient symbol that for thousands of years

is usually associated with sun and power, with the life force and cyclic regeneration – often extended to signify the Supreme Being. In modern times the swastika was monopolized by Hitler as sign of the Nazi party in 1930s.

SWASTIKA Pre-Columbian America variation.

SWASTIKA Viking variation.

SWORD Important and ancient symbol of authority, justice, intellect and light. Emblem of magic. Linked to exceptional virtue and cults of the sword, particularly in Japan and in the religious rituals of the crusades. Carries a ceremonial role, especially to confer knighthoods. Symbol of constancy, and wrath personified, in religious thought it is often equated with wisdom and knowledge.

had been a positive sign of cosmic regeneration was degraded into a political emblem of repression and violence.

TAMBOURINE/ TIMBREL An important ritual object to the Israelites and a Jewish symbol of victory and jubilee.

TAMFOA BEBRE Ghanaian adinkra symbol meaning the importance of learning from the past.

TARGET Modern.

TARTAR Alchemistic, also found on South American rock carvings.

TARTRATE Alchemistic.

TASSELS In 17th-century France the tassel came to represent wealth, prestige and power. As Masonic symbols, the four tassels represent the cardinal virtues. In Catholicism and other religious traditions, the wearing of tassels can symbolize rank.

TAURUS Zodiac sign.

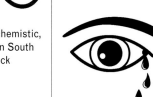

TEARS Symbols of grief or sadness.

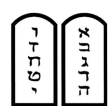

TEETH Primordial symbols of aggressive-defensive power.

TEFILLIN Jewish, leather pouch containing quote from the Torah, strapped to the arm and head.

10

TEN Symbol of perfection, especially in Jewish tradition; symbol for whole of creation for Pythagoreans; and for perfect balance for Chinese.

TEN COMMANDMENTS Jewish.

TEST Alchemistic.

TET OF OSIRIS Also known as the Djed Pillar, is a stylized tree, symbolic of the tamarisk tree that held Osiris's body. It symbolizes sturdiness, stability and the ability of the spirit to break from its earthly bonds and rise towards the heavens. It is equated with the backbone, and possibly also with the penis.

יהוה

TETRAGRAMMATON The four Hebrew letters used to represent the name of God, Yahweh, a name that must not be spoken aloud in the Jewish faith.

THEOSOPHICAL SOCIETY A society founded in the 19th century and still in existence today, whose primary objective is Universal Brotherhood based on the idea that life and all its forms is indivisibly One.

THISTLE Symbol of retaliation; also healing or talismanic powers. Emblem of martyrdom and of Scotland.

THORN Commonly associated with blocks and barriers, whether internal or external. Christ's crown of thorns can be understood as a crown of suffering or as a solar symbol with the thorns representing the rays of the sun emanating outwards. Flying thorns in China were weapons that drove out evil. "A land of thorn and thistles" in the Jewish and Christian traditions referred to soil that was untilled and therefore virginal.

THORN Rune for Th.

THREAD A linking symbol that connects many different states of being to one another, and to a unifying origin. Ariadne's thread linked Theseus between the underworld and the everyday world. Puppet strings link the puppet to the puppet master.

3

THREE The most positive number in symbolism, religious thought, legend, mythology and folklore. The lucky three is a very ancient concept. In Christian thought it has central importance as the doctrine of the Trinity, God the Father, God the Son and God the Holy Spirit, a theology that has forerunners in classical, Celtic and Hindu traditions.

THRONE Traditional symbol of kingship, divine authority and power.

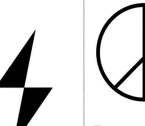

THUNDERBOLT Linked with Nazism, and with the rune for yew, Viking.

TIGER In Asia and India the tiger replaces the lion as the symbol of all that is great and terrible in nature.

TOAD Symbol of death; linked to witchcraft in European traditions; a good luck lunar symbol in China; associated with rain and riches.

TODESRUNE Rune of death.

TODESRUNE Rune of death, variation.

TOMAHAWK Pipe tomahawks were used to seal treaties between different Native American groups. The Algonquian tamahak was ceremonial and a symbol of leadership.

TOMATO The Bambara associate tomato juice with blood, and thus the tomato is considered to have the blood of life, and is the bearer of the foetus.

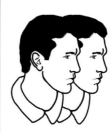

TORCH A symbol of illumination. Its light is born to illuminate passage on a journey. The concept of the flame that is never extinguished is a potent one.

TREE OF LIFE Universal symbol of creation, the tree of life has its roots in the waters of the underworld, its trunk in the earthly world, and its branches in the heavens. Seen as a way of accessing other worlds.

TRIANGLE With horizontal line, element of fire in the Middle Ages.

TRIDENT Symbol of sea power; emblem of Neptune; of ancient Minoan civilization; and later of Britannia.

TUDOR ROSE Emblem of the Tudor royal dynasty created by combining the white rose of York with the red rose of Lancaster.

equilibrium but conflict. Thought of as unlucky in China.

TYR Rune for T.

UMBRELLA See Parasol

TOTEM POLE A symbolic carved pole representing totem animal and guardian spirits of an individual or clan.

TRIANGLE Upside down, element of water. Also negative spectrum of meaning.

TRIANGLE Equilateral, associated with the divine number three, symbol for power, success, prosperity and safety. The Hittites used it for well, good or healthy.

TRIQUETRA A tripartate symbol composed of three interlocked vesica pisces, most commonly used for the Holy Trinity but predates Christianity and was likely a Celtic symbol of the triple goddess or Odin.

TURTLE/TORTOISE Symbol of the whole universe, its shell representing the heavens, and its flat base, earth. Chinese and Amerindian tradition link penile erection with the way the head emerges from its shell.

UNDERWORLD Egyptian hieroglyph.

TREASURE Abundant riches, found rather than earned, have always been a symbol of attainment, and feature in mythologies as reward for the just, or the means to punishment for the wrong-doer.

TRIANGLE Single axis symmetric, variation of equilateral triangle.

TRIANGLE Upside down, with horizontal line, element of earth in the Middle Ages.

TRISKELION Greek word for three-leg, this was found on an Athenian shield used as a competition prize in 500 BC.

TWINS Sign of Gemini, twins are generally symbols of the nature of dualism.

UNICORN Ultimate symbol of chastity, courtly symbol of sublimated desire, Christian symbol of the incarnation.

TRIANGLE With a vertical line, in Hittite hieroglyphics this sign represented the king, the vertical line signifying the unique being inside the triangle, which stood for power and divinity.

TRUMPET Instrument of portent, momentous news or action, used in military, ritualistic and state occasions.

TWO Symbol of duality: division but synthesis, attraction but repulsion,

UR/URUZ Rune, meaning strength, sacrificial animal.

TRIANGLE Pythagorean.

124

URANUS The planet.

URANUS The planet, variation, also morning.

URN/VASE Female symbol, often appearing as emblems of eternal life in art or in funeral rituals.

VENUS The planet.

VENUS The planet, variation.

VESCIA PISCIS Also known as the fish bladder or mystical almond, adopted by Christians from pagan sources to symbolize purity and virginity.

VESSEL/BOWL Alchemical; also ancient Germanic time sign for summer.

VICTORY Christian.

VINEGAR Alchemistic.

VIRGIN MARY A symbol used by the Christian Church to represent the mother of Jesus.

VIRGO Zodiac sign.

VISHNU The Hindu god holds this sign in one of his four hands as a symbol of the whole universe.

VITRIOL Alchemistic.

VITRIOL Early chemistry.

VIVA! See Down with!

VOLKSWAGEN Emblem of the car manufacturer.

WALNUT Judeo-Christian symbol of fertility and longevity.

WAND See Rod

WATER Alchemistic, also modern.

WATER In all times and all cultures; among the earliest Egyptian hieroglyphs; also adopted to signify resistence.

WATER Kabbalism.

WATER Early chemistry.

WATER ELEMENT See Triangle, upside down.

WATER Common in ancient Greece as decoration.

WAX Alchemistic.

WEEK Time sign in alchemy.

WELL The symbolism of the well is commonly associated with qualities of the sacred or of the unconscious; wells are places of knowledge; the source of life; places of healing; wishes or good luck.

WHALE Ark or womb symbol of regeneration, linked with initiation in Africa and Polynesia.

WHEEL Solar image of cosmic momentum, ceaseless change and cyclic repetition; later of power and dominion. Linked with the progress of mankind. Hindu and Buddhist emblem of reincarnation. Western image of fortune and fate.

WHIP Symbol of rulership, judgement and fertility; the flail replaced the whip in Egypt, and the fly whisk in Africa, China and India.

WHITE ARSENIC Alchemistic.

WHITE LEAD Early chemistry.

WIND FURNACE Alchemistic.

WINTER Old Germanic time sign.

WOLF Ambivalent symbol of cruelty, cunning and greed but in other cultures of courage, victory or nourishing care (Roman). Sacred to Apollo and Odin.

WOMAN A common sign in both ancient and modern systems.

WOMAN/FEMALE SEX Egyptian hieroglyphs; also found widely in cave art; associated with growing and genesis implying that woman is the originator of life.

WOOD Alchemistic.

WOOD Alchemistic, variation.

WORLD Tibetan.

WOW FORO ADOBE Ghanaian adinkra symbol for persistence and prudence.

WREATH The first crown – symbol of spiritual or temporal authority – drawing on the symbolism of the circle (perfection) and the ring (continuity).

WYNN Rune for W.

YANTRA STRUCTURE Indian, also sorting in computer usage.

YEAR Time sign, alchemistic.

YIN YANG Chinese symbol for the duality of the universe.

YIN YANG Earliest ideogram for yin yang. Ideogram in the West for the number 10 from latin X; also signifies hourglass.

YOKE Symbol of oppression from Roman times.

YONI Buddhist symbol of the vulva.

ZEUS Sign of the god.

ZEUS God, variation.

ZEUS God, variation.

ZIGZAG

ZINC Alchemistic.

ZODIAC Also known as the ecliptic, the via solis or the way of the sun.

INDEX

ACKNOWLEDGEMENTS

THE ART ARCHIVE: p10t Musée des Antiquités St Germain en Laye/Dagli Orti; p12t British Museum/Dagli Orti; p12b Musée du Louvre, Paris/Dagli Orti; p13t Musée du Louvre Paris/Dagli Orti; p13m Abbey of Novacella or Neustift/Dagli Orti; p14tm Luxor Museum, Egypt/Dagli Orti; p15b Egyptian Museum Cairo/Dagli Orti; p16b Musée du Louvre Paris/Dagli Orti; p17tl National Archaeological Museum Athens/ Dagli Orti; p19 Chateau de Malmaison, France/Dagli Orti; p21t National Museum of Prague/Dagli Orti; p21b Bibliothèque des Arts Décoratifs Paris/Dagli Orti; p27t Taj Mahal, India, Dagli Orti; p36 from George Catlin's illustrations; p42t Buddha, Musée Guimet, Paris/Dagli Orti; p45t Palatine Library Parma/Dagli Orti; p46tr Museo San Marco Florence/Dagli Orti; p46br Musée des Beaux Arts Tours/Dagli Orti; p48t Turkish and Islamic Art Museum Istanbul/Dagli Orti; p49b British Library; p53tl Palazzo Barberini Rome/ Dagli Orti; p52tr; p54t; p55 Musée des Beaux Arts Nantes/Dagli Orti; p66t British Museum; p72b British Library; p74t Venus of Willendorf; p75 Peggy Guggenheim Collection Venice/Dagli Orti.

THE BRIDGEMAN ART LIBRARY: p19tl Museo e Gallerie Nazionali di Capodimonte, Naples, Italy; p19b Louvre, Paris, France, Lauros/Giraudon; p20tl Musee des Antiquites Nationales, St. Germain-en-Laye, France; p26t, Nottingham City Museums and Galleries (Nottingham Castle); p30b Museo Nacional de Antropologia, Mexico City, Mexico, Sean Sprague/Mexicolore; p37t Bibliotheque des Arts Decoratifs, Paris, France, Archives Charmet; p38b Bibliotheque Nationale, Paris, France/ Archives Charmet; p40b Private Collection/Ann & Bury Peerless Picture Library; p47 Prado, Madrid, Spain, Giraudon; p50t Freud Museum, London, UK; p51tr Archives Larousse, Paris, France; p52b Fogg Art Museum/Harvard University Art Museums, USA, Bequest of Grenville L. Winthrop; p56 Johnny van Haeften Gallery, London, UK; p57t Prado, Madrid, Spain; p57b Collection Kharbine-Tapabor, Paris, France; p58b Private Collection; p59 Private Collection/Chris Beetles, London, UK; p70br Private Collection/Chris Beetles, London, UK; p72t Bristol City Museum and Art Gallery, UK; p73t Musee Gustave Moreau, Paris, France.

CORBIS: p20b Richard T. Nowitz; p22bl; p22br Charles & Josette Lenars; p23t DiMaggio/Kalish; p23m Kevin Fleming; p24 Paul Almasy; p25l Charles & Josette Lenars; p25r Margaret Courtney-Clarke; p28t Wolfgang Kaehler; p28b Chris Rainier; p29ct Charles & Josette Lenars; p29bl Michael & Patricia Fogden; p32b; p33t; p34t John Noble; p34b Peter Harholdt; p35b Tiziana and Gianni Baldizzone; p39t Brian A. Vikander; p41t Reuters; p43t Christine Kolisch; p48b Nevada Wier; p52t Close Murray/Corbis Sygma; p53b Elke Stolzenberg; p61b Richard Hamilton Smith; p64t Hulton-Deutsch Collection; p54b David Turnley; p55t Bettmann; p55b Hulton-Deutsch Collection; p66b Archivo Iconografico, S.A.; p67t Anthony Bannister; Gallo Images; p69tl Matthew McKee; Eye Ubiquitous; p69tr; p74m Charles & Josette Lenars; p74b Christie's Images; p76b Murray Andrew/Corbis Sygma; p77b Leonard de Selva; p78b 1661-Drawing of Copernicus' world system, Bettmann; p79t Galileo Galilei before the Inquisition (ca. 1632) by Robert-Fleury, Bettmann.

THE KOBAL COLLECTION: p76t Warner Bros/The Kobal Collection.